Becoming One New Woman in a Journey Through the Books of Ruth and Esther

DR. LEE ANN B. MARINO, PH.D., D.MIN., D.D.

# FEMININE PERSPECTIVES OF GOD

# FEMININE PERSPECTIVES OF GOD

Becoming One New Woman in a Journey Through the Books of Ruth and Esther

### Dr. Lee Ann B. Marino, Ph.D., D.Min., D.D.

Published by:
*Righteous Pen Publications*
*The righteousness of God shall guide my pen*
www.righteouspenpublications.com

All rights reserved. No part of this book may be reproduced or transmitted in any form or by any means, electronic or mechanical, or information storage and retrieval system without written permission from the author.

Unless otherwise noted, Scriptures taken from the **Holy Bible, New International Version ®, NIV® (1984),** Copyright © 1973, 1978, 1984, 2011 by Biblica, Inc.™ Used by permission of Zondervan. All rights reserved worldwide.

All passages marked EXB are from **The Expanded Bible.** Copyright ©2011 by Thomas Nelson. Used by permission. All rights reserved.

All passages marked ESV are taken from the **Holy Bible, English Standard Version®,** Copyright © 2001 by Crossway, a publishing ministry of Good News Publishers. All rights reserved. Used by permission.

All passages marked AMPC are taken from **The Amplified° Bible Classic Edition (AMPC),** Copyright © 1954, 1958, 1962, 1964, 1965, 1987 by The Lockman Foundation. Used by permission. (www.Lockman.org)

All passages marked KJV are taken from the **Holy Bible, Authorized King James Version,** Public Domain.

Cover and interior images in the Public Domain.

Book Classification: Books > Religion & Spirituality > Christian Books & Bibles > Bible Study & Reference > Commentaries > Old Testament > Historical Books.
Books > Religion & Spirituality > Religious Studies > Theology > Feminist.

Copyright © 2022, 2025 by Dr. Lee Ann B. Marino.

ISBN: 1-940197-57-0
13-Digit: 978-1-940197-57-9

Printed in the United States of America.

Toughness doesn't have to come
in a pinstripe suit.
(Dianne Feinstein)[1]

# Table of Contents

Preface.................................................................... vii

Introduction: The Books of Ruth and Esther.................. 1

1 New Beginnings in Great Losses (Ruth Chapter 1)........... 9

2 No Delicate Little Flower! (Ruth Chapter 2).................... 41

3 Do You Want a Boaz or a Naomi? (Ruth Chapter 3)......... 63

4 One New Woman in the Kinsman-Redeemer (Ruth Chapter 4)................................................................. 77

5 The "NO" Heard Round the World (Esther Chapter 1)...... 93

6 Laying Foundations in the Midst of a Conspiracy (Esther Chapter 2)................................................................. 115

7 Here for Such a Time as This (Esther Chapters 3-6).......... 137

8 Celebrating Female Bravery (and All Those Who Helped) (Esther Chapters 7-10)................................................... 167

References................................................................. 195

About the Author........................................................ 201

# PREFACE

THE books of Ruth and Esther are perhaps among the most controversial of all Bible books each in their own way, and both for one common reason: they celebrate a woman's relationship with God, even if she doesn't understand it, narrating such from a female perspective. Sure, we love the idea of Ruth and Esther for a women's conference or to celebrate friendship or virtue, but do we consider the theological virtue of both books, each in their own right? Sometimes, whether deliberately or not, we are quick to give the message that Ruth and Esther are not of the same canonical importance as other Biblical books, delegating them to a role of historical rather than spiritual significance. What does such a message say about how we regard women - and the experiences women have with God?

The books of Ruth and Esther are in the Bible for the very reason they are often disregarded: because they give voice to a woman's experience with God in everyday, ordinary ways that we don't often consider, nor credit. They teach us about women in Biblical times, as well as women right now, showing us how we become a part of the church, but more importantly, the church becomes part of us. Without fanfare or fuss, and without pageantry, loud trumpets, and a need for God to prove Himself, the women of God work onward, proving that the Kingdom of God is truly within.

Ruth and Esther are also stories that feature strong queer theological ideas. Queerplatonic partnerships, eunuchs (either gay, transgender, or asexual), strong female characters, outcasts, and individuals living with the challenges of societal marginalization are a theme in these texts. We can see the relevance of such individuals in God's Kingdom, making room for the "different" as well as the standard.

By looking at these two books through a different lens, we learn much about the way that women interact with God and view their relationship with Him, particularly from a historical perspective. Not challenging to understand or complicated in their message, they remind all of us of a need to live our faith, seeing the spirituality in our everyday life assignments, and recognizing that God doesn't always show up in a huge, grand way, but often as a still, small sense of knowing what to do in difficult situations.

Ruth and Esther show us the power of relationship, both with God and with others. Throughout these two books, we can see how our spiritual lives strengthen our bonds together, even when there is nothing that seems to suggest we ought to find them. Here, bravery isn't just a convenient, cute musing for Indiana Jones movies or Kung Fu fighting scenes. The bravery of faith isn't about politics but about doing the right thing, whether in a personal or a relationship that encompasses far more than your own personal well-being, unto the end of types, shadows, and spiritual points that impact the way we perceive God, even to this very day.

From the most advanced believer to a newer believer looking to better understand spiritual purpose through the Scriptures, Ruth and Esther have something to say to you. It might not roar or scream in your face, but the presence of God is there, in it, just the same as in the rest of the Scriptures. As you learn to recognize God's voice throughout these important books, you will see the church, Christ, and the work of the resurrection, all interconnected, and all in a powerful, life-altering way.

# INTRODUCTION
## About the Books of Ruth and Esther

FOR this book, it's all about the girls, the queer kids, and queerplatonic partnerships: Ruth, Naomi, Vashti, Esther, Mordecai, and Hegai. What types of spiritual realities do these people provide for us? Have you ever looked at the Old Testament and wondered just where the promise of the church is, making it clear? How do we know what God wants us to do, when there is something specific He wants us to do? How do we live our faith in an everyday context? How does our faith dictate what we do when it comes to other people? The books of Ruth and Esther are full of answers to these questions, often in ways we never would have expected. To understand our relationship with God, to see how women often have (and still) view God, and how such a radical shift impacts one's lives, we need look no further than Ruth and Esther. For this reason, we must study Ruth and Esther to understand nine key things:

- To understand God, interaction with God, and faith from both a female and queer perspective.

- To thoroughly un-romanticize any ideas we have about the books of Ruth and Esther and see the way in which the female characters worked hard, labored, and did things that were uncustomary for them to do in their day and time.

- To see the powerful type of the church present in the relationship between Ruth and Naomi.

- To recognize the essence of Gentile and outcast inclusion in the church and see that such has been God's plan from the very beginning.

- To understand the way that women are a type of the church by their very nature, with the power to overcome the enemy.

- To see the importance of the Kinsman-Redeemer (Jesus) as He brings all of us together, as one family.

- To see how both Vashti and Esther were a part of God's plan, and the types of both as John the Baptist and Christ Himself.

- To learn what it means to be "here for such a time as this," celebrating assignments and recognizing the voice of God within in such situations.

- To see the resurrection typed in Purim.

## Position in the Bible

The Books of Ruth and Esther are in a group of five scrolls that are a part of the larger classification of "the Writings." The five small scrolls are the Song of Solomon, Ruth, Lamentations, Ecclesiastes, and Esther. They are classified as such because they are short and are part of Jewish devotional and worship life in different ways. Only Esther and Lamentations are universally read, with the other books taking on cultural importance (and read at different times by different communities of Jews). The Writings are one of the three major divisions of the Hebrew Bible, along with the Torah and the Prophets. There are eleven books in total in the Writings. The complete list of Writings includes Psalms, Proverbs, Job, Song of Solomon, Ruth, Lamentations, Ecclesiastes, Esther, Daniel, Ezra, and 1 and 2 Chronicles (regarded as one book). The writings provide spiritual inspiration and song, express relationship with God and with others, provide prophecy and history, and show us the work of God through often trying and difficult times.

The book of Ruth has long been regarded as a part of Biblical canon, if for no other reason because of its evident antiquity. The book of Esther has a far more controversial position in canonical history. It was the last of the books accepted in the Hebrew canon. There have been many in history that question its authenticity, as the Name of God is never spoken within its contents. This doesn't mean God is not present in Esther, but that it has raised ire with some historians and scholars throughout the centuries.

Different canons place the books of Ruth and Esther in different places within the Bible. In Christian canons, Ruth follows Judges and precedes 1 Samuel; in Syriac Christian tradition it is placed between Ecclesiastes and the Song of Solomon; in Jewish tradition it is placed between the Song of Solomon and Lamentations. In most Christian canons Esther is found between Nehemiah and Job; in Jewish tradition Esther is located between Ecclesiastes and Daniel. There is also a Greek version of Esther, included in the Septuagint and often included among the Deuterocanonicals. It retells the story of Esther along with additional traditions not included in the Hebrew version of the book. There are also Coptic, Ethiopic, and Latin versions of Esther, all displaying the relevance of the text across many cultures.

## Length

The Book of Ruth is four chapters long and the book of Esther is ten chapters long. In Bibles that sometimes number the verses differently, the books of Ruth and Esther remain the same numbering and length, with the content in both remaining the same.

## Authors

The book of Ruth is an ancient text with a long history of disputed authorship. The text itself names no author and gives no indication of one. Traditional attribution is ascribed to the Prophet Samuel. There are those who believe it may have been authored later, and in that instance, the author is unknown. Given its attention to detail, quiet nature, and true female perspective, it is possible its authorship was either by a woman or under the direct influence of a woman during the writing process.

The book of Esther also has no clear author, but Jewish tradition has ascribed its authorship to Mordecai. This appears possible, as Mordecai would have had the connection and insight to Esther to record the happenings as she moved and maneuvered with King Xerxes of Persia.

## About the authors

If the Prophet Samuel was the author of Ruth, we recognize him as a major figure in Biblical history. Samuel was the son of Elkanah and Hannah, dedicated to serve God from the time he was weaned from nursing before he was even born. He worked in the temple at Shiloh, and one night, when he was still very young, heard God call his name. It was Samuel who spent the rest of his life revealing wickedness and calling people unto repentance, selecting governmental leaders, keeping those leaders honest in governance and battle, and representing the word of God among His people. If someone else was the author of Ruth, we don't know anything at all about them.

We know of Mordecai through his important role present in the book of Esther. We can recognize him as Esther's close relative and her guardian, as she was orphaned as a child. He lived in Susa in the province of Persia, which is now Iran. He was a devoted man and sincere in his faith, and refused to engage in any form of idolatry, including bowing before Haman, a government official. Haman got upset, and to retaliate sought to kill all the Jews in the Persian Empire. Mordecai discovered the plot, took it to Esther, and while she worked to overturn this anticipated evil, Mordecai fasted, prayed, and kept his ear to the ground for additional information. After the Jewish victory, Mordecai was placed in authority within the empire and was celebrated for his work.

## **Time written**

If the Prophet Samuel authored Ruth, it would have been written during his lifetime, between 1064 and 1012 BC. There are those who suggest that Ruth might have been authored later, especially because it features a Gentile character and her inclusion within the faith. Those who note this as a source of defending interfaith marriage suggest it might have been authored during the Persian period, between the sixth and fourth centuries B.C.

The book of Esther would be from the Persian period, somewhere around the fourth century B.C. If Esther's work happened during the reign of Xerxes I, the activities of the book would have begun around 482 B.C. and concluded around March of 473 B.C. It would have been written, therefore, sometime after that.

## **Who are Ruth and Esther for?**

Both Ruth and Esther are for all believers. They are for female believers in that they help provide an identification point in spiritual experience; and they are for male believers, in that they give insight into female spirituality and important pinpoints for all believers, both male and female. Women were largely excluded from the public spiritual life of Israel (such as in taking vows, for example), and there was, most likely, question as to whether women could even have a spiritual life or hear from God. Ruth and Esther capture women's spirituality on their terms, in their immediate situation and likeness, and reveal that yes, despite questions, women do have a powerful and important relationship with God. Ruth and Esther also show us humble positions that are insightful for laity and leadership alike. The church is for everybody, and we should avoid temptations to see the church as exclusively institutional. The church is more than just institutional; it is personal, relational, and intimate, like Ruth and Naomi and Mordecai and Esther. In the church we are also family, and that forces us to handle our issues, deal with our griefs and joys, support each other, and work out our personal problems as we go along. If you desire to know more about the church in the Old Testament, spiritual types, and the importance of everyday integrity, Ruth and Esther are short books with a wealth of knowledge, all for you. They clearly capture the spiritual life of the church, as well as spirituality in an everyday sort of context.

Ruth and Esther are also stories representative for God's "queer kids," those who don't quite fit in with gender norms, representations, or identities. We find a queer platonic partnership (the relationship between Ruth and Naomi) central to Ruth and an eunuch, an orphan, and a non-traditional family situation central to the book of Esther. Seeing God work through each one of these individuals, relationships, and situations sends a powerful message not just of inclusion, but relevance among queer persons, communities, and relationships.

## **History**

The book of Ruth covers an unknown time frame, although most believe it took place somewhere during a famine in the time of the Judges. This would put the happenings of Ruth somewhere around the eighth century B.C., although its happenings may have occurred even earlier in time. If it was authored in the Persian period, it would have happened somewhere between the sixth and fourth centuries B.C. Historically speaking, Ruth does not offer much historical data. The genealogy found at the end of the book was most likely added later. It provides information on Ruth's relevance in a spiritual and lineage sense but still does not mention much of the history or time frame surrounding its happenings.

The book of Esther is more of a historical recounting. For that reason, we can estimate more of the historical time frame of its contents. Esther takes place in the royal palace of King Xerxes of Persia, documenting part of his reign. This would place the events of Esther between 483 and 482 B.C., concluding in 473 B.C. Thus, the book of Esther covers approximately a ten-year time span.

## **Context**

The book of Ruth details the story of Ruth, a Moabitess, who is now a widow, and the kindness she showed to her mother-in-law, Naomi, who was also widowed and had lost both of her sons in death. As a Gentile, Ruth had no knowledge of God or understanding of Him but still extended herself to care for and bear the responsibility for her mother-in-law, even returning to Bethlehem with Naomi, leaving her own land and people. Ruth labored and worked hard in the barley fields to provide, and caught the eye of Boaz, a relative of Naomi's. Through diligence, patience, and a whole lot of advice from Naomi, Ruth proposes to Boaz, and in the end, she and Naomi become legal family once again, redeeming the family and becoming one through Boaz, the Kinsman-Redeemer. In Ruth, we see the church: the coming together of Jew and Gentile through one who redeems them, and they create one new family as a result.

The book of Esther tells the story of the Persian Empire

and its leader, King Xerxes, who has successfully conquered many nations and lands under his control. To celebrate, he throws a banquet for six months, culminating with the call of Queen Vashti, who is to come wearing the royal crown and not much else, to parade and dance for his men. When she refuses, she is banished from the Kingdom. After a four-year period, Xerxes decides he will find another wife. Enter Esther, an orphan raised by her relative, Mordecai, who gained great favor with the king's staff and enters the palace in his harem. After earning Xerxes' favor, Esther becomes queen, but without a lot of standing or much to do, as the rules were established at the time. With an ear close to all happenings, Mordecai discovers a plot to exterminate all the Jews by one within the king's leaders, Haman. Most disturbed and concerned, Mordecai goes to Esther (who has not revealed she is a Jew), and she works out a plan to go before the king and save her people from genocide. Through careful steps, Esther is victorious, Mordecai is elevated as a leader in the Persian Empire, and Haman is hanged. The Jews all throughout the province of Persia then go to celebrate Purim, a festival that celebrates all God has done for them, and that He truly takes care of His own.

Throughout Esther, we see types: types of the way maker to come, John the Baptist; of Christ; and of the Resurrection, of a great overcoming, through the work of one woman and those sent to help her. More than just a randomly historical piece, we can see how great character can get us very far in our lives, and how God positions us for a purpose, even if we don't recognize or see what He is doing, to bring about His will, even today.

# CHAPTER ONE
## New Beginnings in Great Losses
## (Ruth Chapter 1)

### Key verses

- **Verses 16-18:** *But Ruth replied, "Don't urge me to leave you or to turn back from you. Where you go I will go, and where you stay I will stay. Your people will be my people and your God my God. Where you die I will die, and there I will be buried. May the LORD deal with me, be it ever so severely, if anything but death separates you and me." When Naomi realized that Ruth was determined to go with her, she stopped urging her.*

- **Verses 20-21:** *"Don't call me Naomi," she told them, "Call me Mara, because the Almighty has made my life very bitter. I went away full, but the LORD has brought me back empty. Why call me Naomi? The LORD has afflicted me; the Almighty has brought misfortune upon me."*

### Words and phrases to know

- **Famine:** From the Hebrew word *ra'ab* which means "famine, hunger, famine (in land, nation)"[1]

- **Moab:** From the Hebrew word *Mow'ab* which means "Moab = 'of his father;' a son of Lot by his eldest daughter; the nation descended from the son of Lot; the land inhabited by the descendants of the son of Lot."[2]

- **Elimelech:** From the Hebrew word *'Eliymelek*, which means "Elimelech='my God is king;' Naomi's husband."[3]

- **Naomi:** From the Hebrew word *No`omiy* which means, "Naomi = 'my delight;' wife of Elimelech, mother of Mahlon and Chilion, and mother-in-law of Ruth and Orpah.[4]

- **Mahlon:** From the Hebrew word *Machlown* which means, "Mahlon = 'sick;' son of Elimelech by Naomi and first husband of Ruth."[5]

- **Chilion:** From the Hebrew word *Kilyown* which means "Chilion = 'pining;' an Ephraimite and son of Elimelech by Naomi and the deceased husband of Ruth (or maybe deceased husband of Orpah).[6]

- **Ruth:** From the Hebrew word *Ruwth* which means "Ruth = 'friendship;' daughter-in-law of Naomi, wife of Boaz, and grandmother of David."[7]

- **Orpah:** From the Hebrew word *`Orpah* which means "Orpah = 'gazelle;' a Moabite woman, wife of Chilion, the son of Naomi, and sister-in- law of Ruth."[8]

- **Mother's home:** From two Hebrew words: *'em* which means "mother; point of departure or division"[9] and *bayith* which means "house; place; receptacle; home, house as containing a family; household, family;

household affairs; inwards (metaph.); temple; on the inside; within."[10]

- **Kindness:** From the Hebrew word *checed* which means "goodness, kindness, faithfulness; a reproach, shame."[11]

- **Bethlehem:** From the Hebrew term *Beyth Lechem* which means "Beth-lehem = 'house of bread (food);' a city in Judah, birthplace of David; a place in Zebulun."[12]

- **Mara:** From the Hebrew word *Mara'* which means "Mara = 'bitterness;' a name that Naomi called herself due to her calamities."[13]

- **Afflicted:** From the Hebrew word *ra`a`* which means "to be bad, be evil; to break, shatter."[14]

- **Barley harvest:** From two Hebrew words: *se`orah* which means, "barley"[15] and *qatsiyr* which means "harvesting; boughs, branches."[16]

## Ruth 1:1-5

**In the days when the judges ruled, there was a famine in the land, and a man from Bethlehem in Judah, together with his wife and two sons, went to live for a while in the country of Moab. The man's name was Elimelech, his wife's name Naomi, and the names of his two sons were Mahlon and Kilion. They were Ephrathites from Bethlehem, Judah. And they went to Moab and lived there.**

**Now Elimelech, Naomi's husband, died, and she was left with her two sons. They married Moabite women, one named Orpah and the other Ruth. After they had lived there about ten years, both Mahlon and Kilion also died, and Naomi was left without her two sons and her**

**husband.**

(Related Bible references: Genesis 19:37, Genesis 24:3-4, Exodus 20:23, Exodus 23:24, Exodus 34:12-16, Leviticus 17:7, Leviticus 19:4, Deuteronomy 2:9, Deuteronomy 4:15-31, Deuteronomy 7:3-4, Deuteronomy 28:38, Judges 2:16, Judges 3:7, Judges 3:30, Ezra 10:2, Nehemiah 13:25-27, Malachi 2:11, 1 Corinthians 7:39, 2 Corinthians 6:14)

The book of Ruth opens much as a story: it sets the background for how things happened. This book doesn't just contain a normal story background, especially considering the Old Testament. It sets up a stage for a story of immigration in the beginning and then another relocation to follow, which sets the stage for later events. In a time long, long ago, when the Judges ruled, there was a great famine in the land of Israel. Much like in the story of Joseph and his brothers (Genesis 41-47), famine had a way of relocating the people of God to different places so they could survive. Much like immigrants of history as well of those of today, circumstances force many to start life somewhere else, cutting their losses and beginning again, sometimes with nothing. These few verses in the book of Ruth show us how things happen, as well as how life becomes normal, once again. As life goes on, families settle in, and as hard times come, happy times also return. The family from Bethlehem: Elimelech, Naomi, Mahlon, and Kilion lived their lives with ups and downs: Elimelech dies first, and then Mahlon and Kilion go on to marry Moabite women, Orpah and Ruth. Naomi was cared for by her sons and daughters-in-law, and their lives had adjusted to their new normal, anticipating happier times and greater futures. Then, about ten years into the family's relocation, Mahlon and Kilion also died.

We don't know what the men died from. There are a few theories out there, many of which to divine judgment. We don't see any evidence of such in the text. It is possible it had something to do with the spread of the famine to where they now lived (which was about 40 miles from Bethlehem) or might have had something to do with battle or difficulty in ancient times. Men have always had higher mortality rates than women due to battles, wars, diseases, and other things they would have encountered that women might have withstood. It is a scientific fact that women have better immunity than men (it is understood from a biological perspective they would have had to care for offspring). Few have tried to write in supporting details to the story that are not supported in fact, but no matter what the circumstances of their deaths might have been, all the men in this family died, leaving the three women: Naomi, Orpah, and Ruth.

These few verses give us a great deal of insight into this family, and their remaining situations after the men died. In the first instance, Elimelech and Naomi and their sons were all Hebrews, of what would later become the Jewish faith (even though it probably wasn't structured at this point like it would be later). They were faithful in their worship of the one true God, even when they departed their own land for one of a surrounding pagan neighbor. We don't know how devout they were (they married foreign women, which raises that question). Orpah and Ruth were Moabites, thus pagans, who were not familiar with the worship of the God of the Hebrews or with those customs. We know from the Scriptures that the Israelites were called to be a different people, upholding different regulations and prohibitive of idolatry:

*You must not use gold or silver to make idols for yourselves; do not worship these gods in addition to Me.*
(Exodus 20:23, EXB)

*You must not bow down to their gods or worship [serve] them. You must not live the way those people live. You must destroy their idols [demolish them], breaking into pieces the stone pillars they use in worship [their pillars].*
(Exodus 23:24, EXB)

*Do not worship [turn to] idols or make statues of gods [cast images] for yourselves [Ex. 20:4-6; Deut. 5:8-10]. I am the Lord your God.*

(Leviticus 19:4, EXB)

*Since the LORD spoke to you from the fire at Mount Sinai [Horeb; 4:10], but you did not see Him [any form], watch yourselves carefully! Don't sin [ruin/destroy/spoil/corrupt yourselves] by making idols of any kind, and don't make statues—of men or women, of animals on earth or birds that fly in the air, of anything that crawls [swarms] on the ground, or of fish in the water below. When you look up at [lift your eyes to] the sky [heavens], you see the sun, moon, and stars, and everything in the sky [all the host of heaven]. But don't bow down and worship them [5:8-9; Ex. 20:4-5], because the LORD your God has made these things [apportioned them] for all people everywhere [32:8]. But the LORD brought you out of Egypt, which tested you like a furnace for melting iron [the iron-smelter; 1 Kin. 8:51; Jer. 11:4], and He made you His very own people [inheritance], as you are now [this day].*

*The LORD was angry with me because of you, and he swore that I would not cross the Jordan River to go into the good land the LORD your God is giving you as your own [an inheritance]. I will die here in this land and not cross the Jordan [34:1-8], but you will soon go across and take that good land. Be careful. Don't forget the Agreement [Covenant; Treaty] of the LORD your God that He made with you, and don't make any idols for yourselves, as the LORD your God has commanded you not to do. The LORD your God is a jealous God [5:9; 6:15; Ex. 20:5; 34:14; Josh. 24:19; Nah. 1:2], like a fire that burns things up [a consuming fire].*

*Even after you have lived [grown old; or become complacent] in the land a long time and have had children and grandchildren, don't do evil things [ruin/destroy/spoil/corrupt yourselves]. Don't make any kind of idol, and don't do what the LORD your God says is evil [what is evil/wrong in the eyes of the LORD your God], because that will make him angry. If you do, I ask heaven and earth to speak [witness] against you this day that you will quickly be removed from this land that you are crossing the Jordan River to take [possess]. You will not live there long after that, but you will be completely destroyed. ²⁷ The LORD will scatter you among the other nations. Only a few of you will be left alive, and those few will be in other nations where the LORD will send [lead] you. There you will worship [serve] gods made by people [human hands], gods made of wood and stone, that cannot see, hear, eat, or smell. But even there you can look for the LORD your God, and you will find Him if you look for Him with your whole being [all your heart/mind and all your inner being]. It will be hard [distressful] when all these things happen to you. But after that you will come back to the LORD your God and obey [hear] Him, because the LORD your God is a merciful God [Ex. 34:6; 2 Chr. 30:9; Neh. 9:31; Ps. 111:4; Joel 2:3]. He will not leave [fail] you or destroy [ruin; spoil] you. He will not forget the Agreement [Covenant; Treaty] with your ancestors [fathers], which He swore [promised] to them. (Deuteronomy 4:15-31, EXB)*

*The Israelites [sons/children of Israel] did what the Lord said was wrong [evil in the eyes/sight of the Lord]. They forgot about the Lord their God and served the idols of Baal [Baals; 2:11] and Asherah [Asherahs; sacred trees or poles dedicated to the goddess Asherah; Deut. 16:21; Judg. 6:25].* (Judges 3:7, EXB)

There were even many verses in the Old Testament regulations that prohibited marriage with those of other groups, for the very reason the Israelites would abandon God, and become idolaters, like those of these other nations:

*That I may make you swear by the Lord, the God of heaven and God of the earth, that you will not take a wife for my son from the daughters of the Canaanites, among whom I dwell, but will go to my country and to my kindred, and take a wife for my son Isaac.*
(Genesis 24:3-4, ESV)

*Take care, lest you make a covenant with the inhabitants of the land to which you go, lest it become a snare in your midst. You shall tear down their altars and break their pillars and cut down their Asherim (for you shall worship no other god, for the LORD, Whose Name is Jealous, is a jealous God), lest you make a covenant with the inhabitants of the land, and when they whore after their gods and sacrifice to their gods and you are invited, you eat of his sacrifice, and you take of their daughters for your sons, and their daughters whore after their gods and make your sons whore after their gods.*
(Exodus 34:12-16, ESV)

*They must not offer any more sacrifices to their goat idols [goat images representing demons; 2 Chr. 11:15; Is. 13:21; 34:14], which they have chased like prostitutes [spiritual infidelity is often likened to marital infidelity; Hos. 1:2]. These rules [statutes; ordinances; requirements] will continue for people from now on [throughout their generations].'*
(Leviticus 17:7, EXB)

*You shall not intermarry with them, giving your daughters to their sons or taking their daughters for your sons, for they would turn away your sons from following Me, to serve other gods. Then the anger of the Lord would be kindled against you, and He would destroy you quickly.*
(Deuteronomy 7:3-4, ESV)

*And Shecaniah the son of Jehiel, of the sons of Elam, addressed Ezra: "We have broken faith with our God and have married foreign women from the peoples of the land, but even now there is hope for Israel in spite of this."*
(Ezra 10:2)

*And I confronted them and cursed them and beat some of them and pulled out their hair. And I made them take an oath in the Name of God, saying, "You shall not give your daughters to their sons, or take their daughters for your sons or for yourselves. Did not Solomon king of Israel sin on*

*account of such women? Among the many nations there was no king like him, and he was beloved by his God, and God made him king over all Israel. Nevertheless, foreign women made even him to sin. Shall we then listen to you and do all this great evil and act treacherously against our God by marrying foreign women?"*
(Nehemiah 13:25-27, ESV)

*Judah has been faithless, and abomination has been committed in Israel and in Jerusalem. For Judah has profaned the sanctuary of the LORD, which He loves, and has married the daughter of a foreign god.*
(Malachi 2:11, ESV)

Even in the New Testament, we find such relationships, while not entirely prohibitive, to be approached with caution:

*A woman must stay with [is bound to] her husband as long as he lives. But if her husband dies, she is free to marry any man she wants, but she must marry another believer [in the Lord].*
(1 Corinthians 7:39, EXB)

*Do not be unequally yoked with unbelievers. For what partnership has righteousness with lawlessness? Or what fellowship has light with darkness?*
(2 Corinthians 6:14, ESV)

Considering this, one might question the entire existence of the book of Ruth as it is the detailing (at least on the surface) of a family that moved and became disobedient to the law they agreed to uphold by virtue of their faith. I think making this kind of a sweeping generalization is a judgment; the family of Elimelech and Naomi relocated for survival purposes, and married women who were available to them, as there probably weren't many Israelite women available. Yet this particular situation makes us curious and investigative as to just what marriage was about in ancient times, and what it meant for this particular family.

Marriage in ancient custom wasn't associated with love and camaraderie as we understand it today. It was the fulfillment of a duty, the continuation of a family, tribe, race (or all of the above), the inheritance of property rights, and above all, an alliance between families, tribes, or clans. Divorce was prohibitive because familial successes were riding on every marriage, which included transference of wealth, property, and assurances of peace or cooperation in times of trouble. If it sounds like a lot of heavy stuff rested on a couple's life together, it certainly did. No matter how great or awful a marriage might have been behind-the-scenes at home, it was customary for couples to stay together. In rare instances of divorce, divorces were always granted to men, and the assumption of the divorce was that the woman in the situation somehow brought reproach to him or his family. When a woman married a man, she went from being the property of her father to the property of her husband, and it was assumed that her identity would, from that point on, assume into the life and understanding of her husband's family.

Elimelech, Naomi, and their sons were foreigners in a foreign land, without access to their own relatives, their own people, and other family members who could have easily arranged marriages for their sons among Hebrew women. The text also seems to indicate that by the time Mahlon and Kilion were ready to marry, Elimelech had also died, thus cutting Naomi off from her husband's family. Now not only was she in a foreign land, but she was also widowed. It's very possible that in arranging marriages for her sons, Naomi considered necessary alliances for familial survival: property acquisition, access to certain land rights or agricultural benefits, and for the continuation of their lineage, now that their father had died. The purpose in their marriages wasn't love or enchantment with idolatrous gods; it was to make sure they all had a fighting chance at survival.

This doesn't change the fact that the story of Ruth challenges many long-held ideals about interfaith marriage, including the possibility that a believer may influence a nonbeliever, rather than always assuming things will follow their course the other way around. The book of Ruth proves that such an influence can be prevalent, as we see no discord or issues of faith between families. If anything, there appears to be a great deal of love and connection between Orpah, Ruth, and Naomi, which would not have been customary in this time frame. The three women lived through unspeakable loss: husbands, sons, and brothers-in-law, all without male heirs to inherit property or continue the family lineage. They were three women alone, in an unforgiving culture, that gave no regard to their grief, because the harshness of their world demanded they now find a way to survive.

### Ruth 1:6-14

**When she heard in Moab that the LORD had come to the aid of His people by providing food for them, Naomi and her daughters-in-law prepared to return home from there. With her two daughters-in-law she left the place where she had been living and set out on the road that would take them back to the land of Judah.**

**Then Naomi said to her two daughters-in-law, "Go back, each of you, to your mother's home. May the LORD show kindness to you, as you have shown to your dead and to me. May the LORD grant that each of you will find rest in the home of another husband."**

**Then she kissed them and they wept aloud and said to her, "We will go back with you to your people."**

**But Naomi said, "Return home, my daughters. Why would you come with me? Am I going to have any more sons, who could become your husbands? Return home, my daughters; I am too old to have another husband. Even if I thought there was still hope for me - even if I had a husband tonight and then gave birth to sons - would you wait until they grew up? Would you remain unmarried for them? No, my daughters. It is more bitter**

***for me than for you, because the LORD's hand has gone out against me!"***

***At this they wept again. Then Orpah kissed her mother-in-law good-by, but Ruth clung to her.***

(Related Bible references: Deuteronomy 14:28-29, Exodus 22:22, Deuteronomy 15:11, Deuteronomy 27:19, Job 19:21, Psalm 132:15, Proverbs 17:17, Proverbs 18:24)

The story shifts from notable grief to opportunity for survival: Naomi got word that the famine of Israel was over, and she prepared to return to her homeland. As she started on her journey, however, her two daughters-in-law, Ruth and Orpah, stood alongside her.

This fact is notable, and bespeaks much about the family's relationship, all on its own. Now that Naomi's sons had died, Ruth and Orpah had no legal nor moral obligation to remain with her. In these times, one of the following would have happened: Ruth and Orpah would have been given in marriage to a sibling or close relative of their deceased spouses, and then their familial property and lineage would have raised up through the name of the deceased; or if there were no remaining relatives for the women to marry, they would have been sent back to their families of origin, hopefully to remarry into a new family. When the men in a family died with no male heirs, that signified the end of the family lineage, thus giving the women in that family no property inheritances, no legal rights, and no way to survive or support themselves. The best hope for women such as Ruth and Orpah was to return to their own biological families, that a male relative might recognize their situation, and as they did not have any children, arrange marriages for them with other men. As they had no children for their husbands before they died, they were better candidates for remarriage than a widow with children (who would have been regarded as being the responsibility of her deceased husband's family, although this was not what always happened).

Naomi, however, was in position to live destitute. She indicates she was past menopause, unable to have any future children. Now that her husband and sons had died, she felt she had nothing to live for. This wasn't mere grief talking; the reality she faced was stark and unpleasant. With no husband or male heirs, she had no property rights, no way to care for herself, and no future. Even though Biblical law contained provision for widows (Deuteronomy 14:28-29, Exodus 22:22, Deuteronomy 15:11, Deuteronomy 27:19), they didn't always receive what they should, and many became paupers or beggars, unless a relative emerged who was willing to see to their care. Remarriage was not impossible for a widow, but because someone in Naomi's case was older, without relatives to arrange a marriage and as she was past child-bearing years, remarriage for her would have been unlikely. She found herself alone, not just in an emotional sense, but in a very real, literal reality.

Naomi's decision to return to Bethlehem was, most likely, more than just because the famine ended, although that does connect to the bigger reason for returning. If things were going well back in Bethlehem, she had the best chance of reconnecting with a relative or connecting with a distant relative for the first time who would be willing to take her in and stand responsible for her care. If she remained in Moab, no such possibility would ever exist.

The story of Ruth continues as Naomi encourages her daughters-in-law to return to their own households, encouraging them to consider their practical futures and stand eligible for remarriage among their own familial group. It was Naomi's greatest stand to wish kindness toward them, hoping that as they had respected her customs and their traditions, they, too, would see the kindness of God, of the God they did not themselves know. By going home to their families, they would be returning to their culture, the gods they worshiped in contrast to the true God, and would resume much of their normal lives, that which they lived, saw, and were an active part of before they married Naomi's sons.

Both Ruth and Orpah were hesitant to leave Naomi and desired to remain with her. They knew what would befall Naomi without help and assistance, and these three women also had a powerful bond of grief and loss that tied them together. Naomi was their only reminder of their deceased husbands, of their lives lived together and of the happy times as well as the difficult times. Leaving meant it was all over, and having to start again is daunting much of the time, as we can see from their experience.

Orpah decides to leave; Ruth decides to stay. Some vilify Orpah for leaving, for choosing to return to what she knew, rather than plowing ahead with Naomi and Ruth to something new. She is used as a picture of what happens when people choose to uphold their past rather than persevere through to the future, but such a label is unfair. Plowing ahead into the future versus the past wasn't a concept women of this era would have had, and Orpah did meet with Naomi's request: to return home and find a new life for herself. Orpah did what Naomi told her to do; she was obedient, respecting both her existing culture and the wishes of her mother-in-law. She wasn't one to challenge the system or do something new. Because of this, Orpah chose a conventional, traditional life. She most likely returned to her mother's house, was remarried to another man (some say her descendants were connected to Goliath, although this is highly unlikely), and lived a life much like the one she'd lived earlier, just with a different man and a different theological system of belief. She'd fulfilled her assignment and obligation, and now that her assignment was completed, she went on to resume a different life somewhere else.

Ruth, however, had a different assignment. If we draw nothing else from the book of Ruth, it should make us keenly aware that God gives assignments to all of us, and we all have the choice as to whether to fulfill them. A God that was foreign to Ruth gave her a directive that even she might not have properly understood. Orpah didn't receive the same directive, which meant she left the picture. All of us, especially those of us who do know God, should pay careful attention to our spiritual assignments. Sometimes God gives us tasks that we don't properly understand, nor can we see the end from the beginning in that specific respect. When we are given those tasks, however, we need to discipline ourselves and see them through.

Both Orpah and Ruth made a decision that changed their lives and led them into new beginnings. Orpah and Ruth also prove that some people serve seasonal positions within our lives. Not every assignment we are given proves to be life-long in its endurance. Just as natural seasons change, so do spiritual ones, as well. Attuning to shifts in our seasons makes for better endurance; it helps us to recognize God's guidance within them; and to know exactly what we should do once we find ourselves in the positions that accompany a change in season. Seasonal shifts might be radical as in the case of Orpah and Ruth, or they might be more subtle, but however they come, we can only attune to hearing God within them if we recognize what they are and come to discover what these seasons are to produce. If we aren't called to it, if our time is up, then it is time to move on to whatever is next. There's no shame in this, in acknowledging it, and in rising to the challenge, to embrace the newness of the season that is set to begin.

## **Ruth 1:15-18**

***"Look," said Naomi, "your sister-in-law is going back to her people and her gods. Go back with her."***

***But Ruth replied, "Don't urge me to leave you or to turn back from you. Where you go I will go, and where you stay I will stay. Your people will be my people and your God my God. Where you die I will die, and there I will be buried. May the LORD deal with me, be it ever so severely, if anything but death separates you and me." When Naomi realized that Ruth was determined to go with her, she stopped urging her.***

(Related Bible references: 1 Kings 11:4-7, 2 Kings 23:1-30, Psalm 45:10,

Psalm 96:5, Ephesians 2:17-22)

It was Naomi's desire, as she understood her culture and the system in place, for her daughters-in-law to return to their homes so they could have and experience life again. We often hear of Ruth and Naomi as great studies in friendship between women, relationships that are to exist between in-laws, and sometimes, should be present among women in church. Yet this passage of Ruth reminds us of some things we often fail to recognize, especially when it comes to theology.

Contrary to the picture we try to paint of Ruth in many Christian circles, Ruth was not a Christian, nor was Ruth a Jew. She was a Moabite, from a mountainous region in what is now modern-day Jordan (lying on the eastern shore of the Dead Sea). The Scriptures reveal to us that Israel and Moab were frequently at odds, which makes the story of Ruth and her integration into a Jewish family that much more fascinating. It reveals to us that by their very nature, Ruth and Naomi are a type of the church. Ruth and Naomi represent the coming together of the Jew and the Gentile to form a new family, a new identity in the Body of Christ, thousands of years before Christ was born.

But this begs the question, just who are the Moabites - and how does the Gentile image of the family fit into this story? Just who were the gods that Naomi was sending her daughters-in-law back to find, and that Ruth decided not to follow and pursue for herself?

As a Moabite, Ruth would have worshipped Chemosh, the national deity of Moab. As many ancient tribes, the Moabites were henotheistic, which means while they were pagan and recognized multiple gods, they favored a particular deity for themselves. They didn't believe this deity was the only deity or the most important among all gods but it had a special relevance to them. Chemosh was associated with the goddess Ashteroth and was like Ba'al in nature. There are those who believe Moloch was the same god as Chemosh, but slightly different in form. Chemosh was a destroyer or subduer, represented by a fish, and with a son named Mesha. Worshippers of Chemosh would have engaged in human sacrifice, seeking to satisfy the deity, keeping him happy and ensuring they would have favorable weather, crops, and general life experience.[17]

If you have ever studied Old Testament cultures, this description of Chemosh probably doesn't sound that extraordinary. Most of the tribes in this particular part of the ancient world were very much alike, combining henotheism with human sacrifice and rather brutal imagery of their deities, which often created a certain brutal nature within their own circles. It was for this reason that the Hebrews were expected to be a different people, refraining from the worship and practices of many of these ancient gods. It wasn't a simple matter of theological disagreements, but the way that those theological disagreements related to different practices and systems. The system of the Hebrews was not compatible with those of their neighbors, and for this reason Chemosh was denounced as an idol by the Biblical prophets. He was often spoken of as the "abomination of Moab."

A few generations after Ruth and Naomi (it's also worth noting one could also argue King David was part Moabite, as Ruth is his great-grandmother), the worship of Chemosh entered Hebrew culture through King Solomon. As marriage was a political endeavor in ancient times, Solomon married many pagan wives in an attempt to forge treaties and alliances with his surrounding neighbors. Over time, he turned to the worship of their gods, specifically Chemosh. The worship of this idol in Israel was later destroyed by King Josiah.

*As Solomon grew old, his wives caused him to follow [led him astray after; turned his heart away after] other gods. He did not follow the Lord completely [His heart was not wholly devoted/faithful to the Lord his God] as his father David had done [the heart of his father David had been]. Solomon worshiped [followed; went after] Ashtoreth, the goddess of* the people of Sidon, and Molech [Milcom], the hated [detestable] god of the Ammonites. So Solomon did what the Lord said was wrong [evil in the eyes/sight of the Lord] and did not [refused to] follow the Lord completely as his father David had done.

On a hill east of Jerusalem [the Mount of Olives], Solomon built two places for worship [high places; 3:2]. One was a place to worship Chemosh, the hated [detestable] god of the Moabites, and the other was a place to worship Molech, the hated [detestable] god of the Ammonites.
(1 Kings 11:4-7, EXB)

Then the king sent, and all the elders of Judah and Jerusalem were gathered to him. And the king went up to the house of the LORD, and with him all the men of Judah and all the inhabitants of Jerusalem and the priests and the prophets, all the people, both small and great. And he read in their hearing all the words of the Book of the Covenant that had been found in the house of the LORD. And the king stood by the pillar and made a covenant before the LORD, to walk after the LORD and to keep His commandments and His testimonies and His statutes with all his heart and all his soul, to perform the words of this covenant that were written in this book. And all the people joined in the covenant.

And the king commanded Hilkiah the high priest and the priests of the second order and the keepers of the threshold to bring out of the temple of the LORD all the vessels made for Baal, for Asherah, and for all the host of heaven. He burned them outside Jerusalem in the fields of the Kidron and carried their ashes to Bethel. And he deposed the priests whom the kings of Judah had ordained to make offerings in the high places at the cities of Judah and around Jerusalem; those also who burned incense to Baal, to the sun and the moon and the constellations and all the host of the heavens. And he brought out the Asherah from the house of the LORD, outside Jerusalem, to the brook Kidron, and burned it at the brook Kidron and beat it to dust and cast the dust of it upon the graves of the common people. And he broke down the houses of the male cult prostitutes who were in the house of the LORD, where the women wove hangings for the Asherah. And he brought all the priests out of the cities of Judah, and defiled the high places where the priests had made offerings, from Geba to Beersheba. And he broke down the high places of the gates that were at the entrance of the gate of Joshua the governor of the city, which were on one's left at the gate of the city. However, the priests of the high places did not come up to the altar of the LORD in Jerusalem, but they ate unleavened bread among their brothers. And he defiled Topheth, which is in the Valley of the Son of Hinnom, that no one might burn his son or his daughter as an offering to Molech. And he removed the horses that the kings of Judah had dedicated to the sun, at the entrance to the house of the LORD, by the chamber of Nathan-melech the chamberlain, which was in the precincts. And he burned the chariots of the sun with fire. And the altars on the roof of the upper chamber of Ahaz, which the kings of Judah had made, and the altars that Manasseh had made in the two courts of the house of the LORD, he pulled down and broke in pieces and cast the dust of them into the brook Kidron. And the king defiled the high places that were east of Jerusalem, to the south of the mount of corruption, which Solomon the king of Israel had built for Ashtoreth the abomination of the Sidonians, and for Chemosh the abomination of Moab, and for Milcom the abomination of the Ammonites. And he broke in pieces the pillars and cut down the Asherim and filled their places with the bones of men.

Moreover, the altar at Bethel, the high place erected by Jeroboam the son of Nebat, who made Israel to sin, that altar with the high place he pulled down and burned, reducing it to dust. He also burned the Asherah. And as Josiah turned, he saw the tombs there on the mount. And he sent and took the bones out of the tombs and burned them on the altar and defiled it, according to the word of the LORD that the man of

God proclaimed, who had predicted these things. Then he said, "What is that monument that I see?" And the men of the city told him, "It is the tomb of the man of God who came from Judah and predicted these things that you have done against the altar at Bethel." And he said, "Let him be; let no man move his bones." So they let his bones alone, with the bones of the prophet who came out of Samaria. And Josiah removed all the shrines also of the high places that were in the cities of Samaria, which kings of Israel had made, provoking the LORD to anger. He did to them according to all that he had done at Bethel. And he sacrificed all the priests of the high places who were there, on the altars, and burned human bones on them. Then he returned to Jerusalem.

And the king commanded all the people, "Keep the Passover to the LORD your God, as it is written in this Book of the Covenant." For no such Passover had been kept since the days of the judges who judged Israel, or during all the days of the kings of Israel or of the kings of Judah. But in the eighteenth year of King Josiah this Passover was kept to the LORD in Jerusalem.

Moreover, Josiah put away the mediums and the necromancers and the household gods and the idols and all the abominations that were seen in the land of Judah and in Jerusalem, that he might establish the words of the law that were written in the book that Hilkiah the priest found in the house of the LORD. Before him there was no king like him, who turned to the LORD with all his heart and with all his soul and with all his might, according to all the Law of Moses, nor did any like him arise after him.

Still the LORD did not turn from the burning of his great wrath, by which his anger was kindled against Judah, because of all the provocations with which Manasseh had provoked him. And the LORD said, "I will remove Judah also out of My sight, as I have removed Israel, and I will cast off this city that I have chosen, Jerusalem, and the house of which I said, My Name shall be there."

*Now the rest of the acts of Josiah and all that he did, are they not written in the Book of the Chronicles of the Kings of Judah? In his days Pharaoh Neco king of Egypt went up to the king of Assyria to the river Euphrates. King Josiah went to meet him, and Pharaoh Neco killed him at Megiddo, as soon as he saw him. And his servants carried him dead in a chariot from Megiddo and brought him to Jerusalem and buried him in his own tomb. And the people of the land took Jehoahaz the son of Josiah, and anointed him, and made him king in his father's place.*
(2 Kings 23:1-30, ESV)

The reality of Ruth's spiritual background should speak to us all the more in her proclamation to Naomi. Ruth clearly picked up on enough of her in-laws' faith to move her to a profound sense of purpose and spiritual realization, desiring to know God firsthand in her own life. Seeing their lives made her realize that something in their spirituality, in their lives, was desirable for her as much as it was for them. This means that Naomi and her family engaged in a sort of evangelism through their lives, without speaking a word, without trying to force them into believing, and without trying to ever convince her that in some way her way of life was inferior.

Frequently read at weddings (although it's worth stating that covenant did exist in forms beside marriage in the ancient world), Ruth's pledge to Naomi is far more than just an expression of human love and interaction. It is a commitment forming a queer platonic partnership, one by which lives are shared without romantic or sexual interest. In Ruth's words, we hear the ultimate promise of the Jew and Gentile coming together (a spiritual queer platonic partnership), becoming one in a way that didn't seem any more possible in Ruth's day than it did in the church's time. It could only come through the work of a secondary party, the work of Christ, bringing us together and making us all family. This love is ultimately the highest aspiration for us in the faith: to remain together, to become one, and for God, the true God, to be our God, as we forsake every false way. No matter what happens, we are together unto death. Even now as believers we know we have the promise of resurrection to bind us together for all eternity. Ruth's words are the very song of the church, of love unbreakable, maintained in eternal life, unity, and a power that cannot be overcome by any force present in this world.

This means the book of Ruth had to feature an interfaith marriage to set the stage for the spiritual type of the church it contains. It's not here to create debate about interfaith marriage, but to show us the promise and placement of the church, present within the heart and mind of God, even years before any of us would have thought it to be a consideration. It is a true story of adoption; of becoming a part of something that might not have been seen in the immediate family concept but was a part of the true sense of God's heart and purpose from the very beginning. For the church to exist, we must see the most profound spiritual interfaith marriage: that of Jew and Gentile, not for one to become the other, but for both to become something else, something different, something new, and something greater and more powerful than they ever can be on their own. We must be a people who is new and different, something never done before, thanks to the work of our Redeemer, Christ Jesus, Himself.

Ruth literally lived her pledge to Naomi, leaving her people, her nation, her identity, and her god once and for all to follow Naomi to a land that would possibly breed hostility toward her, viewing her as an enemy. They had to leave where they were to find their personal redeemer, the one who would bring them back together as family, once again. Doing this means Ruth had to make huge sacrifices, not unlike those Naomi and her family made to leave for Moab a decade earlier. It was Ruth who now had to work hard, to deal with a grieved and embittered older woman, and confront the change that was to come in her life. We, too, as believers, also experience similar issues. We must work hard, deal with older believers who are hardened and embittered by the difficulties of life and confront our own changes as we follow our Redeemer. The road doesn't always seem fair or what we might have hoped it to become. Yet in Ruth, we see the promise that God has a way of working things out, bringing us to a place of redemption through our spiritual process, and in ways we might have never considered.

*Christ came and preached [proclaimed the Good News of] peace [Is. 52:7] to you who were far away from God [far away/off], and to those who were near to God [near; Is. 57:19]. Yes, it is [For; or So that] through Christ we all have the right to come [free access] to the Father in [by] one Spirit.*

*Now you Gentiles are not foreigners or strangers any longer, but are citizens together with God's holy people [the saints]. You belong to God's family [household]. You are like a building that was built [...having been built] on the foundation of the apostles and prophets. Christ Jesus himself is the most important stone [cornerstone; or capstone; Is. 28:16; 1 Cor. 3:11] in that building, and that whole building is joined together in Christ. He makes it grow and become a holy temple in the Lord. And in Christ you, too, are being built together with the Jews [built together] into a place where God lives through the Spirit.*
(Ephesians 2:17-22, EXB)

This reality that we now find in the church, in Christ's body, was a type shadowed years and years earlier in Ruth and Naomi. Long before there were millions of us, there were two: Ruth and Naomi, a Jew and a Gentile, bound by a marriage that no longer even connected them or required them to connect via the laws of the day. They forged a commitment, of their own free will and volition, even after their legal relationship faded into non-existence due to spousal death. Ruth, a Gentile, makes a pledge to her mother-in-law, a Jew, even though there was nothing in society that required such. As Ruth made her commitment to Naomi, she echoed the heart of the church, that eternal bond, that love, that makes us one in Jesus Christ.

## Ruth 1:19-22

**So the two women went on until they came to Bethlehem. When they arrived in Bethlehem, the whole town was stirred because of them, and the women exclaimed, "Can this be Naomi?"**
   **"Don't call me Naomi," she told them. "Call me Mara, because the Almighty has made my life very bitter. I went away full, but the LORD has brought me back empty. Why call me Naomi? The LORD has afflicted me; the Almighty has brought misfortune upon me."**
   **So Naomi returned from Moab accompanied by Ruth the Moabitess, her daughter-in-law, arriving in Bethlehem as the barley harvest was beginning.**

(Related Bible references: 2 Samuel 3:31, Job 5:11, Job 19:21, Psalm 38:6-8, Ecclesiastes 3:2-4, Ecclesiastes 7:2-4, Isaiah 12:1, Isaiah 57:18-19, Isaiah 61:1-3, Jeremiah 9:20, Matthew 5:4, Romans 12:15, 1 Corinthians 15:54, James 4:9)

In the hope and promise of our beloved identity as the church we find a powerful reminder of the realities of life Naomi now faced. Gone for a long time, the women of the town started talking, bringing Naomi face-to-face with her reality. She returned to her own people alone, without her husband or sons, and without the joy that her family life brought to her. Now she had to face those she knew; those who were excited about life. It was too much for her to stand in the face of their happiness when all she wanted to do was sit somewhere and feel her sorrow. Destitute and feeling very much alone, Naomi calls for the women to rename her because her grief was so overwhelming, it took her to where it consumed her being. The name Naomi means "pleasant," and Naomi wasn't feeling particularly pleasant about what had happened to her. Instead of feeling pleasant, Naomi felt overwhelmingly bitter, as if she was punished by God, and that her name should change to Mara (meaning "bitter") to reflect the bitterness that had now been forced upon her.

It's easy to read the book of Ruth and look down on Naomi; to accuse her of being stuck somewhere in time, to say she had no uplifted outlook or that she shouldn't have been so chronically negative. It's also easy to see Ruth as the upbeat, optimistic one and Naomi as the negative Nancy that doesn't see any hope for life. Grief is a complicated, non-binary experience that isn't one thing; it is everything. It's everything resolved and unresolved in a now ended relationship; it's the trauma of death itself; it is the trauma of living in the face of having stared down death.

It is here – in that bitterness – where Naomi introduces us to the spirituality of grief and of the importance of its process, so one can find blessing in life again at a later point in time. Spiritual disciplines are found through the things we go through, not despite them. We don't often consider mourning to be a sacred process in the church today, dismissing it as something negative, associated with negative emotion that does not uplift, or have value. The Bible does not support this view. Recognizing the cycle of life that the ancients were far more in touch with than we are today, the Scriptures have much to say about mourning, and what can come forth from the mourning process.

*Then David said to Joab and to all the people who were with him, "Tear your clothes and put on sackcloth and mourn before Abner." And King David followed the bier.*
(2 Samuel 3:31, ESV)

*He sets on high those who are lowly,*
  *and those who mourn are lifted to safety.*
(Job 5:11, ESV)

*I am utterly bowed down and prostrate;*

all the day I go about mourning.
For my sides are filled with burning,
   and there is no soundness in my flesh.
I am feeble and crushed;
   I groan because of the tumult of my heart.
(Psalm 38:6-8, ESV)

A time to be born, and a time to die;
a time to plant, and a time to pluck up what is planted;
a time to kill, and a time to heal;
a time to break down, and a time to build up;
a time to weep, and a time to laugh;
a time to mourn, and a time to dance.
(Ecclesiastes 3:2-4, ESV)

It is better to go to the house of mourning
   than to go to the house of feasting,
for this is the end of all mankind,
   and the living will lay it to heart.
Sorrow is better than laughter,
   for by sadness of face the heart is made glad.
The heart of the wise is in the house of mourning,
   but the heart of fools is in the house of mirth. (Ecclesiastes 7:2-4, ESV)

I have seen his ways, but I will heal him;
   I will lead him and restore comfort to him and his mourners,
   creating the fruit of the lips.
Peace, peace, to the far and to the near," says the LORD,
   "and I will heal him.
(Isaiah 57:18-19, ESV)

The Lord GOD has put His Spirit in me,
   because the LORD has appointed [anointed] me to tell [bring] the good news to the poor.
   He has sent me to comfort [bind up] those whose hearts are broken,

*to tell the captives they are free,*
  *and to tell the prisoners they are released.*
*He has sent me to announce the time when the LORD will show His kindness [year of the LORD's favor; an allusion to the Year of Jubilee; Lev. 25:10; Luke 4:18-19]*
  *and the time when our God will punish evil people [day of vengeance of our God].*
*He has sent me to comfort all those who are sad [mourn]*
  *and to help the sorrowing [mourning] people of Jerusalem [Zion; location of the Temple; 59:20].*
*I will give them a crown [garland; headdress] to replace their ashes,*
  *and the oil of gladness [joy] to replace their sorrow [mourning],*
  *and clothes [a garment] of praise to replace their spirit of sadness [discouragement; heavy heart].*
*Then they will be called Trees of Goodness [or Oaks of Righteousness],*
  *trees planted by the LORD to show His greatness [glory; manifest presence].*
(Isaiah 61:1-3, EXB)

*Now, O women, hear the word of the LORD;*
*open your ears to the words of His mouth.*
*Teach your daughters how to wail;*
*teach one another a lament.*
(Jeremiah 9:20)

*Blessed and enviably happy [with a happiness produced by the experience of God's favor and especially conditioned by the revelation of His matchless grace] are those who mourn, for they shall be comforted!*
(Matthew 5:4, AMPC)

*Rejoice with those who rejoice, weep with those who weep.*
(Romans 12:15, ESV)

*Grieve, mourn and wail. Change your laughter to mourning*

*and your joy to gloom.*
(James 4:9)

Mourning may not be the most fun aspect of life, but it is a part of the life of every human being, including the believer. As long as we are on this earth, we will participate in the cycle of life: that of birth, life, and death, joy and mourning, happiness and sadness. In mourning, we find a place of spiritual revelation, one that brings us a state of comfort, of learning to let others help us, of learning who we can rely on, and on how deeply the Lord opens Himself up to us in times of grief or sadness. What ultimately comes from mourning is the blessing of God Himself, present in His comfort and extension of Himself, which brings the hope of healing and a new day. In our grief process, we become more self-aware, more purposed and dedicated, and ready to address any issues in our lives where God is not first or where we are missing His presence in our experience. Through grief, we can handle what comes next.

Ruth and Naomi had gone through a period of grieving for at least a year whereby their grief was considered primary. After this point, it was assumed life should resume some normality. Naomi's obvious bitterness reveals to us that sometimes grief doesn't follow our normal, scheduled timetables. We like the idea of "getting over grief," but maybe grief isn't something we "get over." Maybe, just maybe, this is all right. Maybe we learn to live with the game changer that it is and slowly adjust to new life, one that isn't the life we'd hoped to have.

We should never, ever feel guilty for grief or mourning, nor should we attempt to hide it. There will forever be periods in our lives where we are not all right, we are not fine, and through such honesty, we find a more honest place in our lives. In a bigger sense, however, this mourning reveals to us much of the new life, of the death that comes about as we move and transition to new life. For spiritual life to break forth, we must first find death.

*I tell you the truth [Truly, truly I say to you], a grain of wheat must fall to the ground and die to make many seeds [much fruit]. But if it never dies, it remains only a single seed [grain].*
(John 12:24, EXB)

*So when this body that can be destroyed [is perishable/corruptible] will clothe itself with that which can never be destroyed [is imperishable/incorruptible], and this body that dies [mortal] will clothe itself with that which can never die [immortality], then this Scripture will be made true [come to pass]: "Death is destroyed forever [swallowed up] in victory [Is. 25:8]."*
(1 Corinthians 15:54, EXB)

When one encounters grief, it's difficult to imagine a world past the intense sense of loss and life disrupted. There's no sense of anything new; only time standing still. This is, too, how things move in nature. For a grain of wheat to become a plant, it goes through a process by which the grain of wheat dies, becoming something other than what it once was so the plant can grow. It happens gradually; a little at a time, becoming one thing, and then something else. From death comes life by virtue of cycle, but it is a cycle that happens on its own timetable, in its own adjustment. One stage is reached, and then another, and still another still, moving along until death brings forth the fullness of life.

    To recognize life, we must experience and encounter death. To recognize newness of life, we must experience the loss of the old. To recognize good times, we must experience difficult and sad times. Life is not all positive, nor is it all negative. Even the most difficult of lives hold within them the promise of life, and of life experiences that reflect joy and pleasantness. Bitterness does not last forever, nor does the sting that we have been forgotten or misplaced. They aren't sinful states, but realistic ones; living ones, ones that reflect life and all that life sometimes offers, whether it is graceful or cruel. Grief is overcome by joy, because as life goes on, there are many new things discovered to explore and experience, all within the hope and anticipation of the joys of life.

Ruth's commitment to Naomi during this most difficult period in her life shows us the power of spiritual discipline. Naomi and Ruth both went through a period of death. It would be through Ruth's commitment that God would move in their lives to bring them back to joy. It is not for us to hang out with people only when they are happy or replace true spiritual empathy and support with platitudes. Rather than trying to force people to feel joyful when they don't, Ruth and Naomi show us that life comes full circle on its own, without human intervention, as life unfolds according to its own course and its own rhythms. God calls us to be people who grieve with those who grieve, rejoice with those who rejoice, and stand firm in our spiritual commitment, even when it's hard. Ruth was a young woman who now committed to spending her life with her angry, embittered, mother-in-law, a woman who probably didn't see the bright side of anything, was probably not real moved that Ruth had made such a great commitment to her (as people in such a state tend to want to be left alone), and it was probably not a whole lot of fun. Ruth stayed through depression, heartache, tear-filled nights, and moments where, in the midst of her own grief, she had to put herself aside to love her mother-in-law, and discover this God that she often spoke of, even though she now felt He had abandoned and left her alone.

But we never think, nor assume, that Ruth's outlook was always optimistic. Ruth and Naomi were not opposites; they were kindred, platonic partners who needed each other at the lowest points of their lives. Inside of every Ruth - every widow who cries when no one is looking, attempts to approach days with bravery, and does what needs to be done in the face of odds - is a Naomi. The embitterment of life after one has experienced death is unavoidable, no matter how well someone might seem to take it. Whether those feelings are felt in the shadows or in the daylight in front of God and everyone, they are very real as the hard work of life - and grief - begins in the aftermath of loss.

God never abandoned Naomi, and the proof of that is in the commitment Ruth extended toward her, in a spirit of love and family. It was a different kind of family now, and a different sort of experience, that they were in to encounter. As a type for us today, in church, Ruth and Naomi represented a different family, a new one, one that wasn't bound through familial obligation or cultural requirement but was bound through the ties of love that only God could create. As we continue in the book of Ruth, we will see just how God takes sorrow and turns it into joy, as these two women take on the world, one moment at a time, with experiences to come and life to abound.

# CHAPTER TWO
## No Delicate Little Flower!
## (Ruth Chapter 2)

## Key verses

- **Verse 2:** *And Ruth the Moabitess said to Naomi, "Let me go to the fields and pick up the leftover grain behind anyone in whose eyes I find favor."*

- **Verses 8-12:** *So Boaz said to Ruth, "My daughter, listen to me. Don't go and glean in another field and don't go away from here. Stay here with my servant girls. Watch the field where the men are harvesting, and follow along after the girls. I have told the men not to touch you. And whenever you are thirsty, go and get a drink from the water jars the men have filled." At this, she bowed down with her face to the ground. She exclaimed, "Why have I found such favor in your eyes that you notice me - a foreigner?" Boaz replied, "I've been told all about what you have done for your mother-in-law since the death of your husband - how you left your father and mother and your homeland and came to live with a people you did not know before. May the LORD repay you for what you have done. May you be richly rewarded by the LORD, the God of Israel, under whose wings you have come to take refuge."*

- **Verses 19-20:** *Her mother-in-law asked her, "Where did you glean today? Where did you work? Blessed be the man who took notice of you!" Then Ruth told her mother-in-law about the one at whose place she had been working. "The name of the man I worked with today is Boaz," she said. "The LORD bless him!' Naomi said to her daughter-in-law. "He has not stopped showing his kindness to the living and the dead." She added, "That man is our close relative; he is one of our kinsman-redeemers."*

## Words and phrases to know

- **Relative:** From the Hebrew word *mowda`* or *moda`* which means "kinsman, relative."[1]

- **Clan of Elimelech:** From two Hebrew words: *mishpachah* which means "clan; every family; families; family; kinds; relatives; tribes"[2] and *'Eliymelek* which means "Elimelech = 'my God is king;' Naomi's husband."[3]

- **Boaz:** From the Hebrew word *bo'az* which means "Boaz= 'quickness;' an ancestor of David, also a pillar before the temple."[4]

- **Glean:** From the Hebrew word *laqat* which means "to pick up, gather, glean, gather up."[5]

- **My daughter:** From the Hebrew word *bath* which means "daughter."[6]

- **Favor:** From the Hebrew word *chen* which means "favour, grace, charm."[7]

- **Foreigner:** From the Hebrew word *nokriy* which means "foreign, alien."[8]

- **Refuge:** From the Hebrew word *chacah* which means "to seek refuge, flee for protection."[9]

- **Comfort:** From the Hebrew word *nacham* which means "to be sorry, console oneself, repent, regret, comfort, be comforted."[10]

- **Blessed:** From the Hebrew word *barak* which means "to bless, kneel."[11]

- **Kinsman-redeemer:** From the Hebrew word *ga'al* which means "to redeem, act as kinsman-redeemer, avenge, revenge, ransom, do the part of a kinsman."[12]

## Ruth 2:1-9

*Now Naomi had a relative on her husband's side, from the clan of Elimelech, a man of standing, whose name was Boaz.*

*And Ruth the Moabitess said to Naomi, "Let me go to the fields and pick up the leftover grain behind anyone in whose eyes I find favor."*

*Naomi said to her, "Go ahead, my daughter." So she went out and began to glean in the fields behind the harvesters. As it turned out, she found herself working in a field belonging to Boaz, who was from the clan of Elimelech.*

*Just then Boaz arrived from Bethlehem and greeted the harvesters. "The LORD be with you!"*

*"The LORD bless you!" they called back.*

*Boaz asked the foreman of his harvesters, "Whose young woman is that?"*

*The foreman replied, "She is the Moabitess who came back from Moab with Naomi. She said, 'Please let me glean and gather among the sheaves behind the harvesters.' She went into the field and has worked steadily from morning till now, except for a short rest in the shelter."*

*So Boaz said to Ruth, "My daughter, listen to me. Don't go and glean in another field and don't go away from here. Stay here with my servant girls. Watch the field where the men are harvesting, and follow along after the girls. I have told the men not to touch you. And whenever you are thirsty, go and get a drink from the water jars the men have filled."*

(Related Bible references: Leviticus 19:9, Leviticus 23:22, Leviticus 24:19, Deuteronomy 14:29, Deuteronomy 4:17-21, 1 Chronicles 2:11, 1 Timothy 5:1-16)

In a stage drama-like fashion, Ruth chapter 2 opens up with a continuation of the story, now focusing on what life was like for Ruth once she and her mother-in-law established their lives in Bethlehem. Much of Ruth chapter 1 focused on Naomi and her specific loss, and Ruth's massive spiritual and social statement to remain with Naomi and support her (despite having no obligation to do so). Now we have a window into what life was like for Ruth: hard labor. Ruth's commitment to Naomi wasn't a simple one of agreeing to split the rent with an aging widow who had no one else in her life. By declaring her commitment to remain with Naomi, Ruth was committing herself to the life of a widow herself. Being the younger of the two, Ruth would be subject to find provisions for the two of them, which were provided according to Biblical law.

*And the Levite [because he has no part or inheritance with you] and the stranger or temporary resident, and the fatherless and the widow who are in your towns shall come and eat and be satisfied, so that the Lord your God may bless you in all the work of your hands that you do.*
*(Deuteronomy 14:29, AMPC)*

*And you shall rejoice before the Lord your God, you and your son and daughter, your manservant and maidservant, and the*

*Levite who is within your towns, the stranger or temporary resident, the fatherless, and the widow who are among you, at the place in which the Lord your God chooses to make His Name [and His Presence] dwell.*

*And you shall [earnestly] remember that you were a slave in Egypt, and you shall be watchful and obey these statutes.*

*You shall observe the Feast of Tabernacles or Booths for seven days after you have gathered in from your threshing floor and wine vat.*

*You shall rejoice in your Feast, you, your son and daughter, your manservant and maidservant, the Levite, the transient and the stranger, the fatherless, and the widow who are within your towns.*
(Deuteronomy 16:11-14, AMPC)

*You shall not pervert the justice due the stranger or the sojourner or the fatherless, or take a widow's garment in pledge.*

*But you shall [earnestly] remember that you were a slave in Egypt and the Lord your God redeemed you from there; therefore I command you to do this.*

*When you reap your harvest in your field and have forgotten a sheaf in the field, you shall not go back to get it; it shall be for the stranger and the sojourner, the fatherless, and the widow, that the Lord your God may bless you in all the work of your hands.*

*When you beat your olive tree, do not go over the boughs again; the leavings shall be for the stranger and the sojourner, the fatherless, and the widow.*

*When you gather the grapes of your vineyard, you shall not glean it afterward; it shall be for the stranger and the*

*sojourner, the fatherless, and the widow.*
(Deuteronomy 24:17-21, AMPC)

The problem with Biblical law was not within itself, but that like much related to the law, the people of Israel didn't always see their way clear to obeying God's provision on these specific matters. Widows often took a heavy hit, as they were either exploited or not properly cared for by family and society. The law sought to make life as easy and as inclusive as possible for those who wound up transient, often through no fault of their own, without specific provision or means to care for themselves. Ruth and Naomi faced a fate, however, that didn't ensure their safety would be a priority for anyone but themselves. We can see in reading this second chapter that both Naomi and Boaz alike were greatly concerned for Ruth's safety as she gleaned behind the workmen in the fields, and that for a woman to take on hard labor and heavy duty in a largely male world left her a target for assault, rape, mistreatment, or worse. This is an example of how some things never seem to change in our societies, and the fact that people prey on the most vulnerable: immigrants or minority communities, indigenous people, individuals who identify or live outside of society's "desired norms" (LGBTQ, homeless, poverty, women alone) is one of those Biblical exposes that should force us to change our hearts and attune to help protect victims and those who are in desperate times, forced into desperate measures. This isn't to say that rape and sexual assault don't happen among every class of people, because even the Bible certainly proves that it does (Genesis 19, Genesis 34, Deuteronomy 21:10-14, Deuteronomy 22:25-27, Judges 19:22-26. 2 Samuel 13:1-14), but it is to say that those who do without something – something that gives them a certain standing or authority within a society – wind up dealing with far more injustice because societal structures are stacked against them. It is that much harder to prosecute, to prove, to pursue for remedy, or to solve, simply because those who already do without don't have the ability to fight for what is rightfully and morally theirs.

Care for widows was not just a part of the Old Testament law, but also became an important part of provision in the early church, sorting out who had family from who did not, and making sure that those who did have family were properly cared for by their relatives, and those who did not were cared for by the church:

*Do not sharply censure or rebuke an older man, but entreat and plead with him as [you would with] a father. Treat younger men like brothers;*

*[Treat] older women like mothers [and] younger women like sisters, in all purity.*

*[Always] treat with great consideration and give aid to those who are truly widowed (solitary and without support).*

*But if a widow has children or grandchildren, see to it that these are first made to understand that it is their religious duty [to defray their natural obligation to those] at home, and make return to their parents or grandparents [for all their care by contributing to their maintenance], for this is acceptable in the sight of God.*

*Now [a woman] who is a real widow and is left entirely alone and desolate has fixed her hope on God and perseveres in supplications and prayers night and day,*

*Whereas she who lives in pleasure and self-gratification [giving herself up to luxury and self-indulgence] is dead even while she [still] lives.*

*Charge [the people] thus, so that they may be without reproach and blameless.*

*If anyone fails to provide for his relatives, and especially for those of his own family, he has disowned the faith [by failing* to accompany it with fruits] and is worse than an unbeliever [who performs his obligation in these matters].

Let no one be put on the roll of widows [who are to receive church support] who is under sixty years of age or who has been the wife of more than one man;

And she must have a reputation for good deeds, as one who has brought up children, who has practiced hospitality to strangers [of the brotherhood], washed the feet of the saints, helped to relieve the distressed, [and] devoted herself diligently to doing good in every way.

But refuse [to enroll on this list the] younger widows, for when they become restive and their natural desires grow strong, they withdraw themselves against Christ [and] wish to marry [again].

And so they incur condemnation for having set aside and slighted their previous pledge.

Moreover, as they go about from house to house, they learn to be idlers, and not only idlers, but gossips and busybodies, saying what they should not say and talking of things they should not mention.

So I would have younger [widows] marry, bear children, guide the household, [and] not give opponents of the faith occasion for slander or reproach.

For already some [widows] have turned aside after Satan.

If any believing woman or believing man has [relatives or persons in the household who are] widows, let him relieve them; let the church not be burdened [with them], so that it may [be free to] assist those who are truly widows (those who are all alone and are dependent).
(1 Timothy 5:1-16, AMPC)

Looking at Ruth through this lens, the commitment she made to Naomi was quite incredible. It was more than just an emotional commitment; it was also a spiritual one and a physical one, as she made herself responsible for Naomi's care. Ruth pledged to become Naomi's family, even though she didn't have to, even though it was going to require something intense of her, maybe more than she desired to give. This was a whole new world for Ruth: new people, new customs, new ways of living, and we see Ruth coming in and stepping up to her duty, without complaint, without hesitation, and without first stopping to see if someone else could do it. Ruth reminds us of the powerful commitment we should, as the church, make toward those who are in situations with compromised or non-existent provision in this life. We should make a point to care for those who do not have families, who have been abandoned by spouses or parents for whatever the reason, for those who are far away from their native lands, due to immigration or relocation, due to politics or other issues that might be more relevant in our times (children alienated from parents due to being gay or lesbian, for example) or due to some other issue, it is our expressed and stated position to be like Ruth to such individuals. While we may not, due to differences in modern society, be required to provide financial care or provision for such individuals, we are called to stand with them and be the family they do not have, providing encouragement, fellowship, camaraderie, and a sense of love, anchoring, and that feeling of home, even in our modern times. The issues may seem different, but the results are the same; and that calls us, as believers, to be Ruth to someone who doesn't have a family on account of whatever situation brought them to that place, today.

Ruth was now living her commitment as part of this society with laws that specifically prohibited landowners and farmers from picking their crops clean for their own purposes. Old Testament law specified that crops should not be gleaned or gathered from the leftovers of the grain or other produce, after the harvest was over. Rather, harvesters were allowed one shot to run through, gather what they could, and the rest was to be left for widows, orphans, strangers, immigrants, and foreigners living in the land to gather for their own provision. Kind of like having a food bank fund, those who needed these provisions were welcome to gather them, but the catch was they had to do it themselves. This is exactly the work that Ruth set out to do: she followed behind the harvesters in a field, gathering what she could from the barley harvest, gathering up what was left over after they came through to gather what was fully grown and ripe. As God would have it (certainly not luck, by any means) she wound up in the field of Boaz, who was a relative of her deceased father-in-law, Elimelech.

We don't know from Scripture, nor from tradition, just how Boaz was related to Elimelech, or how he factored into their familial position. We do know that he was a landowner and did appear to be wealthy, as he was not forced to work on his own farm in the harvest, with many farmhands and servant girls to perform the work for him. We can also see the character of Boaz in how he handled his workers. He made sure they had water and adequate food and gave them a rest in order to sustain themselves during the labor-intensive harvest. Upon hearing about Ruth, Boaz instructs Ruth to remain in his field, gleaning there, with full provision and permission to gather whatever she could.

Boaz was clearly old enough to be Ruth's father; he even refers to her as "my daughter." In reviewing these chapters of Ruth, there is no evident interest, nor attraction between Ruth and Boaz. Ruth and Boaz were both doing their jobs, working hard and attending to the needs that surrounded them. No one was flirting or showed the slightest interest in the other. Ruth was concerned about surviving and providing for her mother-in-law; Boaz was doing his duty as a close relative of Elimelech, extending familial courtesy and provision by proxy through Ruth. He made sure she had what she needed to survive, and that she would be safe and protected in his fields.

### Ruth 2:10-18

*At this, she bowed down with her face to the ground. She exclaimed, "Why have I found such favor in your eyes that you notice me – a foreigner?"*

*Boaz replied, "I've been told all about what you have done for your mother-in-law since the death of your husband – how you left your father and mother and your homeland and came to live with a people you did not know before. May the LORD repay you for what you have done. May you be richly rewarded by the LORD, the God of Israel, under Whose wings you have come to take refuge."*

*"May I continue to find favor in your eyes, my lord," she said. "You have given me comfort and have spoken kindly to your servant – though I do not have the standing of one of your servant girls."*

*At mealtime Boaz said to her, "Come over here. Have some bread and dip it in the wine vinegar."*

*When she sat down with the harvesters, he offered her some roasted grain. She at all she wanted and had some left over. As she got up to glean, Boaz gave orders to his men, "Even if she gathers among the sheaves, don't embarrass her. Rather, pull out some stalks for her from the bundles and leave them for her to pick up, and don't rebuke her."*

*So Ruth gleaned in the field until evening. Then she threshed the barley she had gathered, and it amounted to about an ephah. She carried it back to town, and her mother-in-law saw how much she had gathered. Ruth also brought out and gave her what she had left over after she had eaten enough.*

(Related Bible references: Exodus 22:21, Exodus 23:9, Leviticus 19:34, 1 Samuel 24:19, Job 34:11, Psalm 112:9, Proverbs 22:9, John 1:5, Philippians 3:20, Hebrews 6:10)

It's obvious from Ruth's response to Boaz's kindness toward

her that she was very aware of her status as a foreigner, an outsider among Jewish society. Not only was she a foreigner, but she was also living as a widow, in a manner that was completely uncustomary for her time in history. No matter how you want to spin it, Ruth was in a situation to stand out. Nothing about her or her actions blended in with those around her. As is customary when this happens, Ruth expected to be treated as an outsider. This was probably because Ruth was, most likely, being treated like her outsider status. She was a young woman caring for an older, embittered, angry woman, with no requirement to do so. People probably talked about her behind her back and wondered why she was doing what she was doing, and Ruth wasn't ignorant of the situation. Just as all of us know when people are running their mouths, so did Ruth. What was a beautiful expression of commitment somehow turned into something else in the wrong mind and mouths, and just as people don't understand our position in the world and what we do, so people didn't understand what Ruth did, either.

*And the light shineth in darkness; and the darkness comprehended it not.*
(John 1:5, KJV)

*For our conversation is in heaven; from whence also we look for the Saviour, the Lord Jesus Christ.*
(Philippians 3:20, KJV)

Being a Christian - when it's done right - can feel a lot like Ruth's experience. We find ourselves as strangers in a strange land, even if we have never departed from our physical location. Being a believer transports us, moving us with the true love of God to another state of being, another way of experience and life, that separates us from those around us. We start out in one place, following the confines of our unique circumstances, following the ways of religion that may not be the ways of God, and doing things the way everyone else does them, for no other reason than we do not know any better. Once God comes into our lives and transforms us (often by calling us out of something), everything seems different. We don't fit in like we used to, and we might find we don't have as much in common with people we knew once upon a time. The light of Christ, at work within us, shines in the darkness – in these difficult, dark places and among difficult people – and it is not understood by them.

Maybe even more relevant than Ruth's awareness of her status was that she didn't expect Boaz to notice or consider her. She wasn't doing anything that she did with the expressed goal or hopes to gain Boaz's attention – or anyone's attention, for that matter. She was simply doing what she knew to be the right thing, moving by instinct, as she was led by God. In both Ruth and Esther, we don't see God as a literal guiding force, directing the women in either book by angelic direction or booming voice; instead, they were following instinct. Someone might argue Ruth and Esther weren't very spiritual for that reason, but it is, in actuality, the opposite. As we can see here in Ruth, her spiritual direction was a part of her everyday life, with no contradiction between the spiritual and the natural. In that direction was focus and was attention to the assignment at hand. Ruth wasn't all over the place, hoping to attract a random man and trying to get attention everywhere she went. She knew what she had to do, and she focused on it, no matter how difficult it might have been.

There's no questioning how difficult these transitional periods can be in our lives and that their difficulties send us wandering, sometimes into places where it is better for us to refrain from going. When we've done something in a hard time, it's tempting to hope that what we do will be rewarded in a tangible sense, whether it's that others praise us for it or that we get something out of it for ourselves. I have heard countless stories of women and men who landed in bad relationships because they started looking for attention in a hard place and time. In these difficult periods, it is even more important that we don't attempt to fill our lives with just anything that comes along so as to avoid any sort of emotional or spiritual discomfort.

Yet while Ruth wasn't looking for anything on her own behalf, she found favor in Boaz's eyes. He knew what she was doing, and no matter what people might have said against her, he recognized the grace of God moving through her unto Naomi's behalf. It was no accident that Boaz took notice, because as a relative of Elimelech, Ruth was stepping up to care for a relative that was no closer in step nor stride than Boaz was to Naomi. She was doing a duty that was not required, and such spoke to him, so much so that he felt responsible to ensure she was able to do what she needed to do. She did her part, and Boaz was to do his part, as well. Notice, however, that there is nothing within Ruth or Boaz that suggested such would end in marriage. Instead, he offered her the same status as a servant girl, a younger woman who would have worked in the process on behalf of the harvest, even though she did not even share this status within their society. She was fed, she was protected from harm, and she was given the opportunity to work all day, gleaning in the field, and bringing home leftovers from the meal she shared with the other workers.

God extends to us much of what Boaz extended to Ruth, simply because He can, He recognizes our need, and He recognizes all we are working to accomplish with Him. God doesn't care our status, the position we might have in this world or in society, how rich or poor we are, or whatever standing might be labeled upon us as members of a specific culture. We might have to work hard, but God sees to it that our burdens are lifted, our work is that much easier, and our ability to do whatever needs to be done reaches its accomplishment. Just as the Holy Spirit's presence came through the trial and difficulty of Christ (and such is represented by wine in places within the Scriptures), the Spirit shall come to us, easing our burdens, filling us up, and bringing us to a place of new comfort, where what we bring back shall be more than enough, and more than we expect.

### Ruth 2:19-23

*Her mother-in-law asked her, "Where did you glean today? Where did you work? Blessed be the man who took notice of you!"*

*Then Ruth told her mother-in-law about the one at whose place she had been working. "The name of the man I worked with today is Boaz," she said.*

*"The LORD bless him!" Naomi said to her daughter-in-law. "He has not stopped showing his kindness to the living and the dead." She added, "That man is our close relative; he is one of our kinsman-redeemers."*

*Then Ruth the Moabitess said, "He even said to me, 'Stay with my workers until they finish harvesting all my grain.'"*

*Naomi said to Ruth her daughter-in-law, "It will be good for you, my daughter, to go with his girls, because in someone else's field you might be harmed."*

*So Ruth stayed close to the servant girls of Boaz to glean until the barley and wheat harvests were finished. And she lived with her mother-in-law.*

(Related Bible references: Leviticus 25:25, Leviticus 25:47-55, Leviticus 27:9-25, Deuteronomy 25:5-10, Hebrews 2:10-13)

Naomi knew from all Ruth brought home that someone – somewhere – had taken notice of her situation and sought to bless her. God was a blessing to Ruth through Boaz, just as God was a blessing to Naomi through Ruth. Everyone did and operated as they were supposed to, and all had enough. There was no lack and no sorrow, and for the first time in this entire scenario, Naomi was able to see that God had not forgotten her.

Paralleling the same realization, this is also the first time in the entire text that Naomi seems to express joy or happiness about anything. She might have been touched by Ruth's commitment to her, but she never expressed much happiness about it; she just didn't argue with Ruth's decision to remain with her. Ruth came all the way to Bethlehem and started a new life with Naomi, but Naomi never seemed to feel blessed by her presence. Now, as Ruth returns, having received favor, we finally see Naomi express a certain level of joy over something. I believe this is because she realized God's hand was in their situation, and while it was easy to assume nothing good would ever happen again after all her loss, Naomi was face-to-face with the promise that she would pull through, and in the end, everything would come to a place where things could be all right again.

Naomi also brings up the reality that Boaz is a relative and has the power to serve as a kinsman-redeemer, or one who can rescue another under the statutes of Old Testament law. The work of the kinsman-redeemer wasn't as heroic as it might sound today. They weren't superheroes but were male relatives who had the legal ability to intervene on behalf of another relative who was in need, in trouble, or in some sort of legal danger. They had the power to redeem property or redeem a person, and in Levirate marriages, they also had the ability to continue lineages or family inheritances by marrying a widow and continuing the family line under the brother's name.

*If your brother has become poor and has sold some of his property, if any of his kin comes to redeem it, he shall [be allowed to] redeem what his brother has sold.*
(Leviticus 25:25, AMPC)

*If a stranger or sojourner with you becomes rich, and your brother beside him becomes poor and sells himself to the stranger or sojourner with you or to a member of the stranger's clan, then after he is sold he may be redeemed. One of his brothers may redeem him, or his uncle or his cousin may redeem him, or a close relative from his clan may redeem him. Or if he grows rich he may redeem himself. He shall calculate with his buyer from the year when he sold himself to him until the year of jubilee, and the price of his sale shall vary with the number of years. The time he was with his owner shall be rated as the time of a hired worker. If there are still many years left, he shall pay proportionately for his redemption some of his sale price. If there remain but a few years until the year of jubilee, he shall calculate and pay for his redemption in proportion to his years of service. He shall treat him as a worker hired year by year. He shall not rule ruthlessly over him in your sight. And if he is not redeemed by these means, then he and his children with him shall be released in the year of jubilee. For it is to me that the people of Israel are servants. They are my servants whom I brought out of the land of Egypt: I am the LORD your God. (Leviticus 25:47-55, ESV)*

*If the vow is an animal that may be offered as an offering to the LORD, all of it that he gives to the LORD is holy. He shall not exchange it or make a substitute for it, good for bad, or bad for good; and if he does in fact substitute one animal for another, then both it and the substitute shall be holy. And if it is any unclean animal that may not be offered as an offering to the LORD, then he shall stand the animal before the priest, and the priest shall value it as either good or bad; as the priest values it, so it shall be. But if he wishes to redeem it, he shall add a fifth to the valuation.*

*"When a man dedicates his house as a holy gift to the LORD, the priest shall value it as either good or bad; as the priest values it, so it shall stand. And if the donor wishes to redeem his house, he shall add a fifth to the valuation price, and it shall be his.*

*"If a man dedicates to the LORD part of the land that is his possession, then the valuation shall be in proportion to its seed. A homer of barley seed shall be valued at fifty shekels of silver. If he dedicates his field from the year of jubilee, the valuation shall stand, but if he dedicates his field after the jubilee, then the priest shall calculate the price according to the years that remain until the year of jubilee, and a deduction shall be made from the valuation. And if he who*

dedicates the field wishes to redeem it, then he shall add a fifth to its valuation price, and it shall remain his. But if he does not wish to redeem the field, or if he has sold the field to another man, it shall not be redeemed anymore. But the field, when it is released in the jubilee, shall be a holy gift to the LORD, like a field that has been devoted. The priest shall be in possession of it. If he dedicates to the LORD a field that he has bought, which is not a part of his possession, then the priest shall calculate the amount of the valuation for it up to the year of jubilee, and the man shall give the valuation on that day as a holy gift to the LORD. In the year of jubilee the field shall return to him from whom it was bought, to whom the land belongs as a possession. Every valuation shall be according to the shekel of the sanctuary: twenty gerahs shall make a shekel."
(Leviticus 27:9-25, ESV)

If brothers dwell together, and one of them dies and has no son, the wife of the dead man shall not be married outside the family to a stranger. Her husband's brother shall go in to her and take her as his wife and perform the duty of a husband's brother to her. And the first son whom she bears shall succeed to the name of his dead brother, that his name may not be blotted out of Israel. And if the man does not wish to take his brother's wife, then his brother's wife shall go up to the gate to the elders and say, 'My husband's brother refuses to perpetuate his brother's name in Israel; he will not perform the duty of a husband's brother to me.' Then the elders of his city shall call him and speak to him, and if he persists, saying, 'I do not wish to take her,' then his brother's wife shall go up to him in the presence of the elders and pull his sandal off his foot and spit in his face. And she shall answer and say, 'So shall it be done to the man who does not build up his brother's house.' And the name of his house shall be called in Israel, 'The house of him who had his sandal pulled off.' (Deuteronomy 25:5-10, ESV)

The work of the kinsman-redeemer existed to provide

tangible evidence of God's work as the true redeemer and Savior of His people. It was God's greatest promise to His people that He would care for them and redeem them from any situation, no matter how impossible or complicated it might have seemed. In particular, God has always expressed Himself as a great protector of those in situations just like Ruth's and Naomi's – those who did not have anyone in the immediate to care for them.

This is also parallel as to Christ as our kinsman-redeemer:

*For it was fitting that He, for Whom and by Whom all things exist, in bringing many sons to glory, should make the founder of their salvation perfect through suffering. For He Who sanctifies and those who are sanctified all have one source. That is why He is not ashamed to call them brothers, saying,*

*"I will tell of your name to My brothers;*
*in the midst of the congregation I will sing your praise."*

*And again,*
*"I will put my trust in Him."*

*And again,*
*"Behold, I and the children God has given me."*
(Hebrews 2:10-13, ESV)

Christ is our brother in the flesh, the One Who sanctified us, and rescued us from sin and the ravages of death and torment on account of His work on the cross. Thus, the work of the kinsman-redeemer also points to the ultimate redemption that humanity finds in Christ. In the story of Ruth, Boaz, the kinsman-redeemer, was a powerful type of Christ, one that was found as Ruth worked hard in the fields, not avoiding her realities, but pursuing them. Yet as Ruth and Naomi are a type of the church, Boaz is a necessary component in that story: we do not have a church if we do not have a redeemer. His position was not to create a fairy-tale like edge to the saga of the century, but to complete the picture of Jew and Gentile coming together as one. No matter how much Jews and Gentiles have tried throughout the centuries to come together on their own, with their own powers and treaties, none have been successful. The only successful unity both can find is through the Redeemer, Christ.

As people, we can try all sorts of projects to bring the church together or to bring people together, in general. We can make up our own rules, establish our own guidelines, form councils, set up dialogue, and talk until we are blue in the face, but it will never work without the power of Christ to redeem us from what ails us. Ruth and Naomi had an ailment: they were poor, they were lost, they were on their own, and they needed someone to step up and do something they could not do for themselves. They did what needed to be done and stayed true to the assignment and issue at hand. Whenever we attempt to take on work or projects that deny our need for divine intervention, they will not go the way we hope them to go. It is better for us to acknowledge our need, to look to God, and to see just how He will specifically work in each and every situation to bring about the unity that is needed. Unity cannot come from any source but God, because He is the original One, the original and all-sufficient, from Whom all life - and all unity - comes forth.

Naomi's mind was, most likely, already considering their impoverished state and a way that Boaz could intervene on their behalf, acting as their redeemer, restoring their status and caring for them. Moving under God's power, even though she probably didn't properly understand it, Naomi knew there was something more in store for their relationship with Boaz, as he had the power to intervene for property, for societal redemption, and even to bring back their family lineage, even though it seemed like it had already died. Encouraging Ruth to remain in Boaz's fields, Naomi knew that staying close to Boaz was something that would be good for them in the long run. Ruth and Boaz weren't on to her plans, but it would be Naomi's persistence, and quick thinking, which would bring them all together as family, once again.

# CHAPTER THREE
Do You Want a Boaz or a Naomi?
(Ruth Chapter 3)

## Key verses

- **Verses 1-4:** *One day Naomi her mother-in-law said to her, "My daughter, should I not try to find a home for you, where you will be well provided for? Is not Boaz, with whose servant girls you have been, a kinsman of ours? Tonight he will be winnowing barley on the threshing floor. Wash and perfume yourself, and put on your best clothes. Then go down to the threshing floor, but don't let him know you are there until he has finished eating and drinking. When he lies down, note the place where he is lying. Then go and uncover his feet and lie down. He will tell you what to do."*

- **Verses 10-14:** *"The LORD bless you, my daughter," he replied. "This kindness is greater than that which you showed earlier: You have not run after the younger men, whether rich or poor. And now, my daughter, don't be afraid. I will do for you all you ask. All my fellow townsmen know that you are a woman of noble character. Although it is true that I am near of kin, there is a kinsman-redeemer nearer than I. Stay here for the night, and in the morning if he wants to redeem, good; let him redeem. But if he is not willing,* *as surely as the LORD lives I will do it. Lie here until morning." So she lay at his feet until morning, but got up before anyone could be recognized; and he said, "Don't let it be known that a woman came to the threshing floor."*

- **Verse 18:** *Then Naomi said, "Wait, my daughter, until you find out what happens. For the man will not rest until the matter is settled today."*

## Words and phrases to know

- **Home:** From the Hebrew word *manowach* which means "resting place, state or condition of rest."[1]

- **Winnowing:** From the Hebrew word *zarah* which means "to scatter, fan, cast away, winnow, disperse, compass, spread, be scattered, be dispersed."[2]

- **Threshing floor:** From the Hebrew word *goren* which means "threshing-floor; barn, barn floor, corn floor, void place."[3]

- **Wash:** From the Hebrew word *rachats* which means "to wash, wash off, wash away, bathe."[4]

- **Perfume:** From the Hebrew word *cuwk* which means "to anoint, pour in anointing."[5]

- **Servant:** From the Hebrew word *'amah* which means "maid-servant, female slave, maid, handmaid, concubine."[6]

- **Corner of your garment:** From two Hebrew words: *paras* which means "to spread, spread out, stretch, break in pieces"[7] and *kanaph* which means "wing, extremity, edge, winged, border, corner, shirt."[8]

- **Woman of noble character:** From two Hebrew words: *chayil* which means "strength, might, efficiency, wealth, army;"[9] and *'ishshah* which means "woman, wife, female."[10]

- **Shawl:** From the Hebrew word *mitpachath* which means "cloak."[11]

- **Empty handed:** From the Hebrew word *reyqam* which means "vainly, emptily."[12]

## Ruth 3:1-6

*One day Naomi her mother-in-law said to her, "My daughter, should I not try to find a home for you, where you will be well provided for? Is not Boaz, with whose servant girls you have been, a kinsman of ours? Tonight he will be winnowing barley on the threshing floor. Wash and perfume yourself, and put on your best clothes. Then go down to the threshing floor, but don't let him know you are there until he has finished eating and drinking. When he lies down, note the place where he is lying. Then go and uncover his feet and lie down. He will tell you what to do."*

*"I will do whatever you say," Ruth answered. So she went down to the threshing floor and did everything her mother-in-law told her to do.*

(Related Bible references: Deuteronomy 25:6, Leviticus 25:25, Ecclesiastes 9:8)

Chapter 3 opens as Naomi reveals her intention to get Ruth and Boaz together. Within the practice of ancient custom, Naomi stepped up to intervene and find Ruth a new spouse, as a male relative would have done for her had she returned to her family of origin. Because people in those days didn't seek out relationships of their own free will and volition, we can see Naomi's intervention was quite necessary, for more than one reason. It was clearly never Ruth nor Boaz's idea, and had Naomi not involved herself in the situation, Ruth and Boaz would, most likely, never have married. Naomi could see the long-term benefit in the situation, even if it wasn't particularly something Ruth or Boaz were interested in pursuing. She knew he was a kinsman-redeemer, their marriage would be of benefit to Ruth, and it would also be of benefit to Naomi. Both she and Ruth would be back within Elimelech's family clan, and that would entitle both of them to legal properties and benefits that otherwise would remain off the table. Naomi's foresight saw potential that would be of benefit to everyone, and she set herself to force the situation that would have gone nowhere without her intervention.

I think this is important because we often meet women who say they are "waiting for their Boaz," but haven't read the details of the story well enough to realize that neither Ruth nor Boaz showed any interest in a personal relationship with one another. Boaz was old enough to refer to Ruth as "my daughter," which meant he didn't even regard himself as a possible or potential suitor for her. They'd had limited contact, and it's obvious that while he did desire to show her favor and extend kindness toward her, Boaz's motives do not display the slightest interest in marriage. While women who make this statement are implying they desire to have a man of wealth and means desire to take care of them, that isn't in the details of this story. Many women appear to pray for a Boaz and then find themselves in a relationship with a man who is uncommitted or disinterested in marriage, not realizing they got exactly what they prayed for. Maybe instead of praying for a Boaz, these women should pray for a Naomi, a woman who can offer guidance and direction in their relationships!

In sincerity, Naomi gave very specific - and direct - advice to Ruth in what she should venture to do next. Naomi could see that neither of them would be willing to make the next move, and Ruth was the one who would have to approach Boaz, because if they waited for him to move, nothing would ever get done. She was to wash and dress herself, prepare and perfume herself, and go to the threshing floor at night, uncover his feet, and wait to see what he does.

The details of this particular passage in Ruth are most interesting, because Ruth literally threw herself at Boaz in the name of marrying him and had the potential to threaten her very life in the process. The threshing floor was a part of ancient custom, and all villages and cities had their own threshing floor, usually located on a rock. The grain would be spread over the rock, and then livestock would walk over the kernels, separating the grain from the chaff. The threshing floor was a place where public matters were often resolved, such as the arrangement of marriages or cases of redemption. It was considered an open place, not a private or personal one, and this is why Ruth was sent to the threshing floor to deal with Boaz. The catch is that women were never, ever, under any circumstances, to be present at the threshing floor at night. Such was considered unsafe and improper for women, due to the work of the livestock and the negotiations that were done on the threshing floor. It might have been where something of this nature would have been sorted out, but it was not something that women did.[13]

Ruth, however, didn't have another option. It would have been improper for them to discuss marriage in the fields and given there was no male relative to negotiate on her behalf, she had to go, herself, for the expressed purpose of surrendering herself to the hope and purpose of his intent to marry her. In the process, however, she risked her very life, because as a woman on the threshing floor, she could have been killed.

## Ruth 3:7-15

**When Boaz had finished eating and drinking and was in good spirits, he went over to lie down at the far end of the grain pile. Ruth approached quietly, uncovered his feet and lay down. In the middle of the night something**

*startled the man, and he turned and discovered a woman lying at his feet.*

*"Who are you?" he asked.*

*"I am your servant Ruth," she said. "Spread the corner of your garment over me, since you are a kinsman-redeemer."*

*"The LORD bless you, my daughter," he replied. "This kindness is greater than that which you showed earlier: You have not run after the younger men, whether rich or poor. And now, my daughter, don't be afraid. I will do for you all you ask. All my fellow townsmen know that you are a woman of noble character. Although it is true that I am near of kin, there is a kinsman-redeemer nearer than I. Stay here for the night, and in the morning if he wants to redeem, good; let him redeem. But if he is not willing, as surely as the LORD lives I will do it. Lie here until morning."*

*He also said, "Bring me the shawl you are wearing and hold it out." When she did so, he poured into it six measures of barley and put it on her. Then he went back to town.*

(Related Bible references: Deuteronomy 25:5, Proverbs 31:30-31, Ecclesiastes 3:13, Jeremiah 31:22, Matthew 17:14-21, 1 Timothy 2:10, 1 Peter 3:4)

Boaz finished his work with the harvest, laying down, when Ruth came in at the middle of the night, uncovered his feet, and laid down, right there. Such was a sign of surrender, of humbling and submitting oneself to another. When he woke up out of his sleep, he noticed Ruth laying at his feet and didn't realize who she was. He was shaken up as it was evident he hadn't invited a woman to the threshing floor, and while pagans were accustomed to prostitutes and sex rites during harvest times, Jews were not. Not recognizing nor realizing who she was or why she was there, he was startled. And as a side note, apparently didn't recognize her, which completely blows any theory out of the water that he held some sort of great romantic attachment to her.

Ruth's words to Boaz were a proposal of marriage, as she was asking him, as their kinsman-redeemer, to marry her, and through marriage "redeem" her. Truthfully, she didn't leave him a lot of choice: By spreading his garment over here, he was covering, or protecting her, and extending to her the familial protection that she needed as a widow in society. There are some who interpret the story of Ruth to imply a certain level of sexual entrapment present, but the Scriptures repeatedly state that Ruth's noble character was recognized by Boaz as well as by all the men of the town, and that when Boaz recognized what Ruth presented, he was willing to step up and do what was required of him within the context of familial culture and honor. She was not running around trying to get attention from anyone and everyone, and despite his advanced age, she still honored culture and recognized what she needed to do to create a proper life for herself.

Ruth answers all questions about whether it is all right for a woman to propose to a man (it's fine), and whether or not it's all right to do what needs to be done, even when it falls outside of the lines of cultural guidelines (it is). What Ruth did wasn't customary, but it was necessary. It is perfectly acceptable to be a woman of faith and a woman who doesn't sit still and wait idly by for things to change around her before moving to action. Isn't that the point of our faith - to move us to step out and do new things? Ruth was never a slave to culture, as we can see throughout her history. She married a man who was not of her culture or faith, she stayed with her mother-in-law even when such wasn't for her to do. She sweated it out in the fields, working to provide for herself and a woman that she had no legal nor moral obligation to care for. Now we see how faith moved Ruth to follow her mother-in-law's advice and step out, making a new life for herself, and connecting the two of them, once again.

The faith of Ruth should inspire all of us to do greater things, to do different things, to do things we never imagined doing or thought possible. Faith should inspire us to take steps outside of the box, outside of the comfortable confines we find ourselves in, and to do whatever it is we need to do to get to a greater and more profound place. It might not be easily understood by others and may cause many to look at us with a raised eyebrow, but faith is something that should bring about a challenge and a change, both within us and in the way we are perceived. What Ruth did was revolutionary not just for herself, but for all women, because she gives us all permission to walk into the power of our faith, as God directs us, even if no one around us understands it.

There is something else, here, however, that is as moving as Ruth's faith and just as important. We can see Ruth's type of the church present in her proposal to Boaz as much as we can see it present in the rest of her life and experience with Naomi. In Jeremiah 31:22 we find a most interesting (and often overlooked) prophecy as relates to the work and purpose of the church:

*How long wilt thou go about, O thou backsliding daughter? for the LORD hath created a new thing in the earth, A woman shall compass a man. (KJV)*

*How long will you waver,*
   *O faithless daughter?*
*For the LORD has created a new thing on the earth:*
   *a woman encircles a man. (ESV)*

*You are an unfaithful daughter.*
   *How long will you wander before you come home [waver]?*
*The LORD has made [created] something new happen in the land:*
   *A woman will go seeking [or protect; or embrace; surround] a man. (EXB)*

This prophecy of Jeremiah was given to Israel (often typed as female) when she, as a nation, was in a backslidden state.

Israel was straight up asked how long this would go on, because there will be a time when something new and important would happen: a woman would be a pursuer, wooer, and protector of a man. This was spoken of as a "new thing" because it wasn't a common role for women to take in their relationships. Here in the book of Ruth we see her compassing Boaz, approaching him as his pursuer, rather than the other way around. It was she who sought out the relationship because it was necessary and desirable for her. By doing so, Ruth took on this specific role that the church fulfills for Christ, as part of our call and command to participate in a "new thing." We are the guardians, pursuers, and protectors of our Lord through the church, carrying the Gospel, and working actively to do this work in this world, this side of heaven.

Ruth did what she had to do. The reality of Boaz, however, is that he was hesitant to take on the responsibility of Ruth, no matter how noble or honorable he might have found her to be in her character. There were probably many reasons for his hesitancy. We have no indication Boaz was looking to get married at whatever point of life he was at, particularly to a woman who was younger than he was. He wasn't interested in the responsibility of Ruth, particularly from a marital perspective, or serving as a kinsman-redeemer in the family. Getting married wasn't in Boaz's plan, but it was what was right, and it was in God's plan. Boaz could recognize, no matter how hesitant he was, that more was at stake here, but he still waited to see if a closer kinsman-redeemer (most likely younger) was willing to step in and fulfill the role. If he was, Boaz would let him step up, and if not, Boaz would fulfill his responsibility toward the family. It might not make for a great love story of the ages, but it does prove that when faith meets obligation, faith always touches and transforms to bring about something beautiful among those who least expect it.

Boaz was willing to make a sacrifice, thus securing his type of Christ in the Old Testament. It might not have been what he wanted to do, but it was what was necessary for this family and, by extension, for his own familial honor. This is so much more poignant and relevant theologically than turning the story into a wild romance novel. The fact that Ruth and Boaz were not madly in love shows just how much of a commitment the two of them made for the continuation of their familial line and their survival. Boaz extended a different kind of love to Ruth and Naomi – an unselfish love, an *agape* love, that sought the highest good and the greatest benefit for both. A romance novel, no, but the love of the ages present in their relationship, a divine, holy, and redemptive love, yes. It points us to the love of God through Christ and reminds us that even in our most difficult states, God is there to redeem and love us through and never sends us back empty-handed.

Returning to her mother-in-law, Ruth did not come back empty-handed, either. Moved by her great faith and boldness, Boaz sent Ruth back with enough barley to supply need for both her and her mother-in-law. The specified measurement was added later, and in reality, there is no way Ruth could have carried back six measures of barley in her shawl or outer garment. The imagery refers to an overflow, to a filling of emptiness, which would come to play through Ruth and Boaz's marriage. This overflowing, providing more than enough, would impact Naomi as well as Ruth, as their lives prepared to change forever.

*And when they came to the crowd, a man came up to him and, kneeling before Him, said, "Lord, have mercy on my son, for he has seizures and he suffers terribly. For often he falls into the fire, and often into the water. And I brought him to Your disciples, and they could not heal him." And Jesus answered, "O faithless and twisted generation, how long am I to be with you? How long am I to bear with you? Bring him here to me." And Jesus rebuked the demon, and it came out of him, and the boy was healed instantly. Then the disciples came to Jesus privately and said, "Why could we not cast it out?" He said to them, "Because of your little faith. For truly, I say to you, if you have faith like a grain of mustard seed, you* will say to this mountain, 'Move from here to there,' and it will move, and nothing will be impossible for you." (Matthew 17:14-21, ESV)

Ruth chapter 3 is essentially a continuation of Ruth's incredible faith, coming to learn about a God that she didn't know for herself, but Who blessed her honor and faithfulness in a world as she navigated through the many things she couldn't visibly see, but trusted to be there. Throughout the Scriptures and much of Christian history, people fell into situations that they just couldn't see their way through. They might have seemed to be impossible, and in looking that situation over, didn't see any way that things could happen. Yet Jesus tells us if we have faith that is the size and likeness of a mustard seed – that small – incredible things can happen for us. Such is proven in Ruth, in her life, her willingness to step out, to do what was different, and notice that in her walk of faith, she was never left empty-handed. God never left her forsaken, and we can trust that He will never leave us forsaken, either. We just need to be willing to be bold – be different – and step out in our faith.

## **Ruth 3:16-18**

**When Ruth came to her mother-in-law, Naomi asked, "How did it go, my daughter?"**
    **Then she told her everything Boaz had done for her and added, "He gave me these six measures of barley, saying, 'Don't go back to your mother-in-law empty handed.'"**
    **Then Naomi said, "Wait, my daughter, until you find out what happens. For the man will not rest until the matter is settled today."**

(Related Bible references: Genesis 49:18, Psalm 27:14, Psalm 31:24, Psalm 33:18, Psalm 37:5, Romans 8:28)

Ruth reported back the success of the evening, and Naomi encouraged Ruth to wait. There's a part of every story we could live without...waiting. In this particular instance, waiting was important and essential to the outcome of the story. Boaz had to handle things within order, and Ruth and Naomi had to wait. Just...wait.

*Lord, I wait for your salvation [or victory].*
(Genesis 49:18, EXB)

*Wait for [Hope in] the Lord's help. Be strong and let your heart be brave, and wait for [hope in] the Lord's help.*
(Psalm 27:14, EXB)

*All you who put your hope in [wait for] the Lord be strong and brave [let your heart be courageous].*
(Psalm 31:24, EXB)

*But the Lord looks after [eye of the Lord is on] those who fear Him, those who put their hope [wait on Him] in His love [loyalty; covenant love].*
(Psalm 33:18, EXB)

Waiting is an essential aspect of the exercise of faith, as things don't tend to happen as quickly as we might like them to move along. God's time is not our time, and in waiting, we realize that it is ultimately the Lord Who comes through for us in each situation. As we wait, we develop a sense of patience, or of active working our faith, continuing in the good things that we have done, while we look to and believe for better things to come. As Ruth and Naomi waited for their kinsman-redeemer, they symbolically typed the waiting of the Savior, Christ, to come for everyone's ultimate redemption. Yet people had to wait - four thousand years - for Him to come, and in the meantime, they discovered more about God and His nature and intent toward them. Ruth knew her God, knew Him in a way that many others around her who might have had the written law did not. As more of

God's plan unfolds for her, she would find herself in an amazing place, prepared and ready to join an entirely new lineage.

# Chapter Four
## One New Woman in the Kinsman-Redeemer
## (Ruth Chapter 4)

### **Key verses**

- **Verses 9-10:** *Then Boaz announced to the elders and all the people, "Today you are witnesses that I have bought from Naomi all the property of Elimelech, Kilion and Mahlon. I have also acquired Ruth the Moabitess, Mahlon's widow, as my wife, in order to maintain the name of the dead with his property, so that his name will not disappear from among his family or from the town records. Today you are witnesses!"*

- **Verses 13-15:** *So Boaz took Ruth and she became his wife. Then he went to her, and the LORD enabled her to conceive, and she gave birth to a son. The women said to Naomi: "Praise be to the LORD, Who this day has not left you without a kinsman-redeemer. May he become famous throughout Israel! He will renew your life and sustain you in your old age. For your daughter-in-law, who loves you and who is better to you than seven sons, has given him birth."*

## **Words and phrases to know**

- **Elders:** From the Hebrew word *zaqen* which means "old, old (of humans), elder (of those having authority)."[1]

- **Sandal:** From the Hebrew word *na`al* or *na`alah* which means "sandal, shoe."[2]

- **Witnesses:** From the Hebrew word *`ed* which means "witness."[3]

- **Ephrathah:** From the Hebrew word *'Ephraath* which means "Ephrath or Ephratah = 'ash-heap: place of fruitfulness;' a place near Bethel where Rachel died and was buried; another name for Bethlehem; wife of Caleb."[4]

- **Perez:** From the Hebrew word *Perets* which means "Perez or Pharez = 'breach;' twin son with Zarah of Judah by Tamar and ancestor of two families of Judah, the Hezronites and Hamulites; from the Hezronites came the royal line of David and Christ."[5]

- **Tamar:** From the Hebrew word *Tamar* which means "Tamar = 'palm-tree;' widow of Er, the son of Judah; fiancée of Shelah, another son of Judah; wife of Judah and mother of Pharez and Zerah."[6]

- **Judah:** From the Hebrew word *Yehuwdah* which means "Judah = 'praised;' the son of Jacob by Leah; the tribe descended from Judah the son of Jacob; the territory occupied by the tribe of Judah; the kingdom comprised of the tribes of Judah and Benjamin which occupied the southern part of Canaan after the nation split upon the death of Solomon."[7]

- **Obed:** From the Hebrew word *Abad* which means "Obed='worshiper;' Grandfather of David, son of Ruth and Boaz."[8]

- **Jesse:** From the Hebrew word *Yishay* which means "Jesse = 'I possess;' son of Boaz and the father of king David."[9]

- **David:** From the Hebrew word *David* or *Daviyd* which means "David = 'beloved;' youngest son of Jesse and second king of Israel."[10]

## Ruth 4:1-12

*Meanwhile Boaz went up to the town gate and sat there. When the kinsman-redeemer he had mentioned came along, Boaz said, "Come over here, my friend, and sit down." So he went over and sat down.*

*Boaz took ten of the elder of the town and said, "Sit here," and they did so. Then he said to the kinsman-redeemer, "Naomi, who has come back from Moab, is selling the piece of land that belonged to our brother Elimelech. I thought I should bring the matter to your attention and suggest that you buy it in the presence of these seated here and in the presence of the elders of my people. If you will redeem it, do so. But if you will not, tell me, so I will know. For no one has the right to do it except you, and I am next in line."*

*"I will redeem it," he said.*

*Then Boaz said, "On the day you buy the land from Naomi and from Ruth the Moabitess, you acquire the dead man's widow, in order to maintain the name of the dead with his property."*

*At this, the kinsman-redeemer said, "Then I cannot redeem it because I might endanger my own estate. You redeem it yourself. I cannot do it."*

*(Now in earlier times in Israel, for the redemption and*

transfer of property to become final, one party took off his sandal and gave it to the other. This was the method of legalizing transactions in Israel.)

So the kinsman-redeemer said to Boaz, "Buy it yourself." And he removed his sandal.

Then Boaz announced to the elders and all the people, "Today you are witnesses that I have bought from Naomi all the property of Elimelech, Kilion and Mahlon. I have also acquired Ruth the Moabitess, Mahlon's widow, as my wife, in order to maintain the name of the dead with his property, so that his name will not disappear from among his family or from the town records. Today you are witnesses!"

Then the elders and all those at the gate said, "We are witnesses. May the LORD make the woman who is coming into your home like Rachel and Leah, who together built up the house of Israel. May you have standing in Ephrathah and be famous in Bethlehem. Through the offspring the LORD gives you by this young woman, may your family be like that of Perez, whom Tamar bore to Judah."

(Related Bible references: Genesis 38:1-30, Leviticus 25:25, Numbers 26:20, Deuteronomy 25:7, 1 Chronicles 2:4, Matthew 1:3)

Ruth chapter 4 might be the end of the story of Ruth (in the immediate sense) but it opens the door to an entirely new sense and presence of Ruth's hope and life in the eternal. As the chapter opens, Boaz begins the long, complicated, and involved process to act as the kinsman-redeemer to Naomi and Ruth. Because there was someone else who was eligible to serve as kinsman-redeemer first (meaning he was a closer relative), Boaz had to ensure in front of witnesses that the eligible candidate was not interested in assuming the position of kinsman-redeemer before Boaz had the option to step up and act in the role of kinsman-redeemer himself.

The process was complicated to ensure property rights remained within a designated family. As a secondary point, the complications also ensured members of a family were not being swindled, mistreated, or taken advantage of in some way. In this instance, the property was in the trust of Naomi's in-laws who had died (not Naomi herself, as she was female). To ensure the property would remain among the family of Elimelech and their familial lineage would continue, Boaz had to prove himself and clarify there were no other potential people to step up and claim the property. As much as it sounds like this was a big dispute over land (because in many ways it was), it was also about the continuation of a family line that had no chance of restoration without Boaz's intervention. All the male relatives of the family were long dead, and there was no hope for new sons or new male relatives from Naomi and Ruth on their own.

In both a spiritual and literal sense, Boaz's marriage to Ruth was to revive what was lost and bring back to life that which was dead. By acquiring Ruth in the redemption, Boaz committed himself to marry Ruth and raise any resulting children as if they were part of Mahlon's direct line. This means that, legally speaking, Boaz's children would not be considered as his own, but as Mahlon's. This would ensure they could inherit the redeemed property and that the family name would not die out, even though Mahlon died before Ruth had children with him. In such an arrangement, we find the kinsman-redeemer not just a restorer of property to the living, but a type of the resurrection, as through him, that which was dead comes back to life again.

The kinsman-redeemer who was first in line to serve for familial redemption was interested until he discovered Ruth's position in the acquisition. Having to raise up children for another man would have interfered with his own estate, perhaps because he already had heirs of his own. This was more common than one might think. While modern society looks on such arrangements as some sort of free relationship, many avoided levirate marriages because they would interfere with their own inheritances or heirs. Not interested in the property and in Ruth, he removed his sandal and gave it to Boaz as a symbol of the transaction.

The sandal was a symbol of authority, and removing the sandal showed the widow's freedom from this male relative's authority and claim over the woman as a wife and over the property as the potential inheritor.[11]

With the "tossing of the shoe," as Jewish custom called it, Boaz was free to serve as the kinsman-redeemer, declared and seen in the presence of all the elders and witnesses present. He would perform his responsibility to continue the family line. In excitement and anticipation, the people present declared Ruth to become as Rachel and Leah, building up the house of Israel, building their standing in Ephrathah (a fruitful place), which was another name for Bethlehem, and that the offspring might be like the family of Perez.

Most of us recognize Rachel and Leah, the two wives of Jacob. It was the two of them who served as matriarchs for Israel, mothers of children who would become the heads of the twelve tribes of Israel. But who was this family of Perez? Truth be told, we don't know a whole lot about them. Perez was the name of a Biblical individual, a male, who was the product of Judah and Tamar. He was also the twin brother of Zerah. The name literally means to "bust forth" or "breach." As was customary in Old Testament times, his name speaks about the conditions surrounding his birth.[12]

*At that time Judah withdrew from his brothers and went to [lodge with] a certain Adullamite named Hirah.*

*There Judah saw and met a daughter of Shuah, a Canaanite; he took her as wife and lived with her.*

*And she became pregnant and bore a son, and he called him Er.*

*And she conceived again and bore a son and named him Onan.*

*Again she conceived and bore a son and named him Shelah.*

[They were living] at Chezib when she bore him.

Now Judah took a wife for Er, his firstborn; her name was Tamar.

And Er, Judah's firstborn, was wicked in the sight of the Lord, and the Lord slew him.

Then Judah told Onan, Marry your brother's widow; live with her and raise offspring for your brother.

But Onan knew that the family would not be his, so when he cohabited with his brother's widow, he prevented conception, lest he should raise up a child for his brother.

And the thing which he did displeased the Lord; therefore He slew him also.

Then Judah said to Tamar, his daughter-in-law, Remain a widow at your father's house till Shelah my [youngest] son is grown; for he thought, Lest perhaps [if Shelah should marry her] he would die also, as his brothers did. So Tamar went and lived in her father's house.

But later Judah's wife, the daughter of Shuah, died; and when Judah was comforted, he went up to his sheepshearers at Timnath with his friend Hirah the Adullamite.

Then it was told Tamar, Listen, your father-in-law is going up to Timnath to shear his sheep.

So she put off her widow's garments and covered herself with a veil, wrapped herself up [in disguise], and sat in the entrance of Enaim, which is by the road to Timnath; for she saw that Shelah was grown and she was not given to him as his wife.

When Judah saw her, he thought she was a harlot or devoted

prostitute [under a vow to her goddess], for she had covered her face [as such women did].

He turned to her by the road and said, Come, let me have intercourse with you; for he did not know that she was his daughter-in-law. And she said, What will you give me that you may have intercourse with me?

He answered, I will send you a kid from the flock. And she said, Will you give me a pledge (deposit) until you send it?

And he said, What pledge shall I give you? She said, Your signet [seal], your [signet] cord, and your staff that is in your hand. And he gave them to her and came in to her, and she became pregnant by him.

And she arose and went away and laid aside her veil and put on the garments of her widowhood.

And Judah sent the kid by the hand of his friend the Adullamite, to receive his pledge from the woman's hand; but he was unable to find her.

He asked the men of that place, Where is the harlot or cult prostitute who was openly by the roadside? They said, There was no harlot or temple prostitute here.

So he returned to Judah and said, I cannot find her; and also the local men said, There was no harlot or temple prostitute around here.

And Judah said, Let her keep [the pledge articles] for herself, lest we be made ashamed. I sent this kid, but you have not found her.

But about three months later Judah was told, Tamar your daughter-in-law has played the harlot, and also she is with child by her lewdness. And Judah said, Bring her forth and let *her be burned!*

*When she was brought forth, she [took the things he had given her in pledge and] sent [them] to her father-in-law, saying, I am with child by the man to whom these articles belong. Then she added, Make out clearly, I pray you, to whom these belong, the signet [seal], [signet] cord, and staff.*

*And Judah acknowledged them and said, She has been more righteous and just than I, because I did not give her to Shelah my son. And he did not cohabit with her again.*

*Now when the time came for her to be delivered, behold, there were twins in her womb.*

*And when she was in labor, one baby put out his hand; and the midwife took his hand and bound upon it a scarlet thread, saying, This baby was born first.*

*But he drew back his hand, and behold, his brother was born first. And she said, What a breaking forth you have made for yourself! Therefore his name was called Perez [breaking forth].*

*And afterward his brother who had the scarlet thread on his hand was born and was named Zerah [scarlet].*
(Genesis 38:1-30, AMPC)

Perhaps the most notable thing we can recognize in parallel between Boaz and Ruth's situation and the birth of Perez is the fact that Perez was born out of the rejection of levirate marriage rather than the execution of it. As a "filler" story of sorts that gives us an idea of just how much time had elapsed between Genesis 37 and Genesis 39, Genesis 38 tells the story of Judah's family, the patriarch of the tribe of Judah. Judah's son, Er, was married to Tamar, who was righteous in the face of her wicked husband. He was so wicked, in fact, that he died for his wickedness. Then Onan,

Judah's other son, was told to marry Tamar in a levirate marriage. Onan knew the offspring from the marriage wouldn't be his, so he practiced a primitive form of birth control (the "withdrawal method") to make sure she didn't get pregnant. Out of Onan's disobedience he also died, because what he did equated to wickedness. Instead of doing something to right the situation, Judah became concerned he would experience the loss of another son. He urged Tamar to live as a widow until his youngest son was old enough to continue the levirate tradition. Tamar returned to her family home, continued to live as a widow, and in the meantime, Judah's wife died.

Tamar comes to find out that Judah's youngest son grew up and she was not given as his wife. She disguises herself as a prostitute, wearing a veil, to seduce Judah. In a scenario that was both strategic and extremely easy, Tamar was successful, securing a goat from his flock and proof she was with Judah (through his signet seal, cord, and staff). She was also successfully pregnant, secured through her husband's line, to acquire property and resolve need through them. When Judah found this out, however, he was furious, saying she should be put to death by burning - not realizing he was the father. His own items were presented to him, and humbled, Judah acknowledges that Tamar was righteous, because she did what she had to do - and he did not do what was required under the law.

Tamar's experience is more than just good writing or drama to entice with exciting storytelling. It is a true story of a woman who was left with no options and did just what she had to do to preserve her own family line and seal her own protection and lineage. It was she who was righteous, rather than the men in her life. Man after man left her abandoned and mistreated, whereas they were the ones who came from a favored lineage and she, herself, was the outsider. Much like Ruth, who although not mistreated by her spouse or her in-laws, Tamar had the common experience of abandonment without heirs. They both had property and rights that needed to be upheld, and through their offspring would come great blessing.

Tamar's encounter with Judah left her the mother of twins: Perez, who was born first, and Zerah, who was born second. They thought Zerah would be the first born, but it was Perez who was born first, breaking forth what he made for himself. As the firstborn, he would have carried on Judah's lineage with his own life. He was also, as part of the tribe of Judah, part of Boaz's ancestry, and therefore, part of David's ancestry, and ultimately, the ancestry of Jesus Christ.

Yet the faith for all this started with a woman - Tamar - and her determination to have what she knew was for her. The same is true of Ruth - her story started in the face of horrible grief, of loss and a sense of abandonment - to persevere through, doing what had never been done before, knowing what she knew she had to do, to bring her to the place where her life, her first husband's memory was restored, and her life came full circle, back to a place of fulfillment. Ruth had to persevere through to find the blessing that would bring her to where she was. Thus, in the pursuit of Tamar, we find the blessing of Perez. Now in Ruth we find the blessing of Obed. Through Perez, we see the connection between two women who were part of the same lineage of faith, all on their own: in the absence of male involvement, without being native believers, both acting righteously and doing the right thing, all because they learned to follow the leading of a God they came to know through their circumstances.

## **Ruth 4:13-22**

***So Boaz took Ruth and she became his wife. Then he went to her, and the LORD enabled her to conceive, and she gave birth to a son. The women said to Naomi: "Praise be to the LORD, Who this day has not left you without a kinsman-redeemer. May he become famous throughout Israel! He will renew your life and sustain you in your old age. For your daughter-in-law, who loves you***

*and who is better to you than seven sons, has given him birth."*

*Then Naomi took the child, laid him in her lap and cared for him. The women living there said, "Naomi has a son." And they named him Obed. He was the father of Jesse, the father of David.*

*This, then, is the family line of Perez:*

*Perez was the father of Hezron,*
*Hezron the father of Ram,*
*Ram the father of Amminadab,*
*Amminadab the father of Nahshon,*
*Nahshon the father of Salmon,*
*Salmon the father of Boaz,*
*Boaz the father of Obed,*
*Obed the father of Jesse,*
*and Jesse the father of David.*

(Related Bible references: Genesis 46:12, Numbers 26:21, 1 Chronicles 2:5, 2 Chronicles 2:12, Isaiah 46:4, Matthew 1:3-5, Luke 1:58, Luke 3:32-33, Galatians 4:1-7)

In the book of Ruth, we find an entire story that depicts the hope and promise of the church. We find four Gospels in the Bible that tell of the story of Christ, and in Ruth, we find four chapters. The whole Gospel message, of life and hope, of renewal of life and the promise of good things to come despite the bad that happens, is found in the book of Ruth. We see the completion of life, death, and then life again, raised to something new in the face of what was perceived to be an end. Somewhere, some way, Ruth's story reminds us that life has a way of finding us again, just like God has a way of finding us when we think there is no way up from here. Two women who were lost in grief, lost in hopelessness, and with no one to call on for their own have now come to a place of restoration and hope.

Yet there is a message in here that we probably miss, and that is one of the "fullness of time." For Ruth to meet

Boaz, for Naomi to realize he was connected to her deceased husband's family, for Obed to ever be born, Ruth had to remain with Naomi, the two had to come to Bethlehem, Ruth had to happen upon Boaz's field for harvest, and Ruth had to follow Naomi's advice unto seeking out Boaz's hand for marriage. The entire story plays out with an intimate and important connection to divine timing that cannot be rushed, nor ignored. God's timing is God's timing, and walking that sight through with patience and diligence is perhaps one of the greatest victories every believer can come to achieve.

*Now I say, That the heir, as long as he is a child, differeth nothing from a servant, though he be lord of all;*

*But is under tutors and governors until the time appointed of the father.*

*Even so we, when we were children, were in bondage under the elements of the world:*

*But when the fulness of the time was come, God sent forth His Son, made of a woman, made under the law,*

*To redeem them that were under the law, that we might receive the adoption of sons.*

*And because ye are sons, God hath sent forth the Spirit of His Son into your hearts, crying, Abba, Father.*

*Wherefore thou art no more a servant, but a son; and if a son, then an heir of God through Christ.* (Galatians 4:1-7, KJV)

Just as the birth of Christ in this world was part of appointed timing, so too is everything that impacts movement and growth in our spiritual lives. Just as Ruth called herself "servant" and later Boaz called her "wife," so we hear God call us "sons," "daughters," and "heirs in His promise. This favor of God is found in all our lives, thanks to the fullness of time.

As Ruth and Boaz marry, Ruth gives birth to Obed. It is at this point in the story that Boaz seems to fade into the background, largely because his purpose was fulfilled. He was the bond to bring these two women back together as lawful family, uniting our type of the church through the kinsman-redeemer. Wherever the church is, we also find Christ, and the redemptive work of Boaz was definitely a type of Christ. As a bonus - or perhaps we can say a most evidential one - Through the lineage of Christ, we find Ruth, thanks to her marriage to Boaz. In their marriage, and their subsequent union, we find Christ, our true spiritual Redeemer. Yet many still wonder, where is Boaz? We honestly don't know, but Jewish tradition often states that Boaz died shortly after Obed's conception or birth. Given he was much older than Ruth, such is a plausible option. He married, he sired a child, and the lineage was secure. If he died, there would be no question as to the inheritance. Naomi, Ruth, and Obed would be set for their lives, and now the newness of their lives was complete.

Obed was brought to Naomi, to be raised as if he was her son, a true blessing and continuation of life, thanks to the intervention of their kinsman-redeemer. Yet as Boaz was no longer literally in the picture, it is not an accident that these two women remained behind, rearing up the powerful lineage and doing the practical and spiritual work to raise Obed. We are in this world to be the church, and to do the practical and spiritual work of Christ. As a loving, nurturing place, one that protects our spiritual lineage, we can see such created by the risk and love of two women, who, without knowing it, were nurturing and continuing the life and promise of the Messiah to come.

In the lineage of Jesus Christ, we find five women, two of which are relevant to Ruth's story: Tamar, mother of Perez and Zerah, and Ruth, mother of Obed.

*Judah was the father of Perez and Zerah.*
   *(Their mother was Tamar [Gen. 38].)...*

*Salmon was the father of Boaz.*
   *(Boaz's mother was Rahab [Josh. 2].)*
*Boaz was the father of Obed.*
   *(Obed's mother was Ruth [Ruth 4:13-22].)*
*Obed was the father of Jesse.*
(Matthew 1:3,5, EXB)

Ruth and Tamar, being of common circumstance and line, remind us that despite life's difficulties, we have a way of finding God right where He reaches out to us. This doesn't mean we should stay where we are, but that we should move to a greater place where He can reveal Himself to us and take us to new levels and dimensions of understanding. No matter our origins, we have a place in God's family, as we live out this experience as His church, the heirs according to His promise. We, too, are the sons and daughters of Ruth and Tamar, and influenced by the faith of Naomi, right down to this present age. That is a lineage to be proud of, and to see life amidst death, light amidst the darkness, and the transformation of anything difficult, common, or unexpected by God's grace, working within, among, and through us as the Kingdom of God is here.

# CHAPTER FIVE
## The "NO" Heard Round the World
### (Esther Chapter 1)

### Key verses

- **Verses 4-8:** *For a full 180 days he displayed the vast wealth of his kingdom and the splendor and glory of his majesty. When these days were over, the king gave a banquet, lasting seven days, in the enclosed garden of the king's palace, for all the people from the least to the greatest, who were in the citadel of Susa. The garden had hangings of white and blue linen, fastened with cords of white linen and purple material to silver rings on marble pillars. There were couches of gold and silver on a mosaic pavement of porphyry, marble, mother-of-pearl and other costly stones. Wine was served in goblets of gold, each one different from the other, and the royal wine was abundant, in keeping with the king's liberality. By the king's command each guest was allowed to drink in his own way, for the king instructed all the wine stewards to serve each man what he wished.*

- **Verses 10-12:** *On the seventh day, when King Xerxes was in high spirits from wine, he commanded the seven eunuchs who served him - Mehuman, Biztha, Harbona, Bigtha, Abagtha, Zethar and Carcas - to* bring him Queen Vashti, wearing her royal crown, in order to display her beauty to the people and the nobles, for she was lovely to look at. But when the attendants delivered the king's command, Queen Vashti refused to come. Then the king became furious and burned with anger.

- **Verses 19-20:** "Therefore, if it pleases the king, let him issue a royal decree and let it be written in the laws of Persia and Media, which cannot be repealed, that Vashti is never again to enter the presence of King Xerxes. Also let the king give her royal position to someone else who is better than she. Then when the king's edict is proclaimed throughout all his vast realm, all the women will respect their husbands, from the least to the greatest."

## Words and phrases to know

- **Xerxes:** From the Hebrew word '*Achashverowsh* or '*Achashrosh* which means "Ahasuerus = 'I will be silent and poor;' title of the king of Persia, probably Xerxes."[1]

- **Susa:** From the Hebrew word *Shuwshan* which means "Shushan or Susa = 'lily;' the winter residence of the Persian kings; located on the river Ulai or Choaspes."[2]

- **Persia:** From the Hebrew word *Parac* which means "Persia = 'pure' or 'splendid;' the empire Persia; encompassed the territory from India on the east to Egypt and Thrace on the west, and included, besides portions of Europe and Africa, the whole of western Asia between the Black Sea, the Caucasus, the Caspian and the Jaxartes on the north, the Arabian desert, the Persian Gulf and the Indian Ocean on the south; the people of the Persian empire."[3]

- **Media:** From the Hebrew word *Maday* which means "Media or Medes or Madai = 'middle land;' a people descended from the son of Japheth and who inhabited the territory of Media; land inhabited by the descendants of Japheth; located northwest of Persia proper, south and southwest of the Caspian Sea, east of Armenia and Assyria, and west and northwest of the great salt desert of Iram."[4]

- **Banquet:** From the Hebrew word *mishteh* which means "feast, drink, banquet."[5]

- **Queen Vashti:** From two Hebrew words: *Vashtiy* which means "Vashti = 'beautiful;' the queen, wife of Ahasuerus, whom he divorced for disobeying his orders"[6] and *malkah* which means "queen."[7]

- **Eunuchs:** From the Hebrew word *cariyc* or *caric* which means "official, eunuch."[8]

- **Wise men:** From the Hebrew word *chakam* which means "wise, wise (man)."[9]

- **Women:** From the Hebrew word *'ishshah* which means "woman, wife, female."[10]

- **Despise:** From the Hebrew word *bazah* which means "to despise, despised; be careless; treat with contempt; regard as despicable; despise, disdain."[11]

- **Respect:** From the Hebrew word *yeqar* which means "price, value, preciousness, honour, splendour, pomp."[12]

- **Husbands:** From the Hebrew word *ba`al* which means "owner, husband, lord."[13]

- **Ruler:** From the Hebrew word *sarar* which means "to be or act as prince, rule, contend, have power, prevail over, reign, govern."[14]

## Esther 1:1-3

***This is what happened during the time of Xerxes, the Xerxes who ruled over 127 provinces stretching from India to Cush: At that time King Xerxes reigned from his royal throne in the citadel of Susa, and in the third year of his reign he gave a banquet for all his nobles and officials. The military leaders of Persia and Media, the princes, and the nobles of the provinces were present.***

(Related Bible references: Daniel 5:28, Daniel 11:2, Romans 12:1-2, 1 Peter 2:4-12)

Much as the book of Ruth opens, the book of Esther opens to set the scene, providing us with information to help set the stage for what comes to pass later in the book. Unlike much of the Bible, this particular book takes place in Susa (now known as Shush), an ancient near eastern city located in Persia, or modern-day Iran, under the Achaemenid Dynasty of the Persian Empire. It is one of the most important cities of the Persian Empire and beyond Persia, of the Near East in ancient times. Susa is only mentioned in two other places in the Bible: once in Nehemiah and once in Daniel. The setting for Esther is important because it was an important seat of history during the story's ten-year backdrop. It was a time of Jewish occupation when Israel was under Persian rule. It also shows what life was like for Jews in nations other than Israel and Judah in an Old Testament setting, namely living under Persian rule and custom, outside of a native understanding of a homeland.

This is most relevant because it means the rulers mentioned in Esther were not Jewish. Xerxes and Vashti, as well as all the ruling men of the province, were not Jewish. The empire itself was known for its extensive tolerance and respect for religious differences, but this does not change the fact that the main characters of the empire were not, themselves, of the Jewish faith. What they would have likely acknowledged as their own was the religion of Zoroastrianism, or better known among its practitioners as Mazdayasna, an ancient Persian faith that was monotheistic in nature, following the worship of Ahura Mazda, a singular god who was the creator of all things. Ahura Mazda was omniscient, omnipotent, omnipresent, unchanging, and the source of all good. They believed in a dualistic understanding, recognizing an equally powerful deity, Angra Mainyu, who was responsible for death and all evil. The religion was first taught by Zoroaster (also known as Zarathustra), considered to be a prophet among adherents of the religion, who lived his life as a polytheistic worshiper until he had a spiritual vision when he was about thirty years old. In it, he saw the presence of Ahura Mazda and six spirits known as the Amesha Spentas (Holy Immortals). During the encounter, Zoroaster asked many questions and learned what he perceived to be the truth, all of which became the foundations of the Zoroastrian religion. Overall, Zoroastrianism upholds a belief in fire as sacred, in sacred purification rituals, against proselytizing, and in the importance of fatherhood and the dead left to be decayed by the elements and eaten by vultures. Their scriptures are known as the Avesta, containing the Gatha hymns, and the younger Avesta, containing details and myths on the religion.[15]

Even though the Persians were largely monotheistic, this did not make them the same as the Jews and does not mean their god was the same as the Lord God Jehovah of the Old Testament. It is also possible that those of the government stature had additional pagan elements inserted here and there, reflecting of cultural polytheism as part of their cultural experience. It doesn't mean that paganism was a driving or dominating force, but that as part of being in such a diverse place, there were influences present, particularly of those who had traveled to different places and were familiar with different customs. It's been said that while the Persians did not worship statues, there were traces of older gods and goddesses from surrounding cultures, such as Anahita (a water deity), Mullissu (goddess wife of Ashur), Mithra (divinity of light), and Urania, the daughter of Zeus known as a muse (most likely influenced by Greek culture). Xerxes I was also Pharaoh over Egypt, and thus the government officials and leaders of the nation would also have exposure and influence from the Egyptian polytheistic worship strains, as well.[16]

So, for Esther to appear on the scene of the Persian government by virtue of divine placement was quite revolutionary and important, indeed. She was a Jew living in a foreign land, not unlike the situation of Elimelech and Naomi and their family in Moab. Even though Esther was most likely born in Persia, she was still a believer in a foreign land that worshiped false gods and embraced practices unlike her own. She and those closest to her were in a situation to practice and live their faith amongst cultures and beliefs that were not like hers.

I've heard many arguments among Christians today of the impossibility for them to live their faith in a secular world that doesn't support their beliefs. If we go all the way back to the beginning, this is exactly what God has always asked His people to do. From the calling out of Noah to build an ark, to Abraham being called from his homeland, to Moses living among the Egyptian hierarchy, to the times where the Hebrews were forced to live captive to their neighbors due to idolatry, to Esther living in Persia, to the first Christians living among pagans and enduring persecution, God has always called his people out and expected that, through His leading and guidance, they would be a set apart people, uniquely called to stand out from those around them by their love of God and love and conduct for one another.

*So [Therefore] brothers and sisters, since God has shown us great mercy, I beg [urge; appeal to] you to offer your lives [selves; bodies] as a living sacrifice to Him. Your offering must be only for God [holy] and pleasing to Him, which is the spiritual [or authentic; true; or appropriate; fitting; or rational; reasonable] way for you to worship. Do not be shaped by [conformed to; pressed into a mold by] this world [age]; instead be ·changed within [transformed] by a new way of thinking [or changing the way you think; the renewing of your mind]. Then you will be able to ·decide [discern; test and approve] what ·God wants for you [is God's will]; you will know what is good and pleasing to Him and what is perfect.* (Romans 12:1-2, EXB)

*Come to Him [then, to that] Living Stone which men tried and threw away, but which is chosen [and] precious in God's sight.*

*[Come] and, like living stones, be yourselves built [into] a spiritual house, for a holy (dedicated, consecrated) priesthood, to offer up [those] spiritual sacrifices [that are] acceptable and pleasing to God through Jesus Christ.*

*For thus it stands in Scripture: Behold, I am laying in Zion a chosen (honored), precious chief Cornerstone, and he who believes in Him [who adheres to, trusts in, and relies on Him] shall never be disappointed or put to shame.*

*To you then who believe (who adhere to, trust in, and rely on Him) is the preciousness; but for those who disbelieve [it is true], The [very] Stone which the builders rejected has become the main Cornerstone,*

*And, A Stone that will cause stumbling and a Rock that will give [men] offense; they stumble because they disobey and disbelieve [God's] Word, as those [who reject Him] were destined (appointed) to do.*

*But you are a chosen race, a royal priesthood, a dedicated nation, [God's] own purchased, special people, that you may set forth the wonderful deeds and display the virtues and* perfections of Him Who called you out of darkness into His marvelous light.

Once you were not a people [at all], but now you are God's people; once you were unpitied, but now you are pitied and have received mercy.

Beloved, I implore you as aliens and strangers and exiles [in this world] to abstain from the sensual urges (the evil desires, the passions of the flesh, your lower nature) that wage war against the soul.

Conduct yourselves properly (honorably, righteously) among the Gentiles, so that, although they may slander you as evildoers, [yet] they may by witnessing your good deeds [come to] glorify God in the day of inspection [when God shall look upon you wanderers as a pastor or shepherd looks over his flock].
(1 Peter 2:4-12, AMPC)

We either believe this is our reality, or we do not. There should be no question in our minds as to its accuracy, as it has been the posture God's people have had to take throughout history. Thus, it makes most sense - and most poignant for insight purposes - that we open the door to Esther by recognizing her station and situation in life. Both she and Ruth alike were trying to survive in harsh conditions, later finding their way into royal places. She was a Jew who was not just led by God but positioned by God to be in an uncomfortable state of her life, surrounded by people who did not believe as she did and did not understand her beliefs. They were a nation, an empire, with an agenda, at the peak of their identity, and sought to expand that territory as far and wide as possible - as well as seek out ways to maintain it.
    It was no simple feat to maintain an empire as large as the Persian Empire at this point in history. For their time and place in history, however, the Persians ran their empire very

well and were noted for their accomplishments in communication and structure. The text indicates the book was written under the rule of King Xerxes (also known as King Ahasuerus in some translations), who we assume to be King Xerxes I of Persia. From what we know of him in history, he was a powerful military leader, ruling the empire of Persia at its greatest point. The Persian Empire reigned from India to Cush, in over one hundred and twenty-seven different provinces. It was the largest empire in history, up to that point in time. Proud of his accomplishments and now back home, off the battlefield, it was his desire to throw a banquet, in his honor, for those who were present in the province.

**<u>Esther 1:4-8</u>**

*For a full 180 days he displayed the vast wealth of his kingdom and the splendor and glory of his majesty. When these days were over, the king gave a banquet, lasting seven days, in the enclosed garden of the king's palace, for all the people from the least to the greatest, who were in the citadel of Susa. The garden hand hangings of white and blue linen, fastened with cords of white linen and purple material to silver rings on marble pillars. There were couches of gold and silver on a mosaic pavement of porphyry, marble, mother-of-pearl and other costly stones. Wine was served in goblets of gold, each one different from the other, and the royal wine was abundant, in keeping with the king's liberality. By the king's command each guest was allowed to drink in his own way, for the king instructed all the wine stewards to serve each man what he wished.*

(Related Bible references: Proverbs 23:31, Ecclesiastes 10:17, Isaiah 24:20, Ezekiel 28:5, Joel 1:5, Romans 13:13, 1 Corinthians 6:10, Ephesians 5:18, Revelation 17:2).

We learn this was no ordinary banquet, however. This was

the biggest banquet any of us could imagine, and it went on for one hundred and eighty days, or about six months. That means for six months, people far and wide came to witness, experience, and see how great Xerxes was, and celebrate the splendor of the empire he'd built. Xerxes had a party, for himself, every single day, for six months. Six months of having to hear about how wonderful he was, what a powerful ruler he was, why he was such a great guy, why everyone should follow his leadership and governing powers, and on and on and on about Xerxes.

As if six months of this wasn't enough, a high feast was held immediately after, to continue in the celebration of all that Xerxes was and had done. This one was held in the gardens, which were a special rarity to display the ability to care for and maintain such elaborate sights. No expense was spared for this banquet, as can be seen in the expense of linen, purple material, silver rings, furniture out of gold and silver, pavements of costly stones, and plenty of wine - as much wine as anyone desired or wanted - flowed liberally, all making an additional (as they'd already been drinking for six months) drunken, sloppy mess, all in tribute to Xerxes. He was in no way a type of Christ, or anyone godly. He was a pagan man, living in a pagan way, celebrating himself in pagan manner, not behaving honorably, but according to his belief and style.

The Bible has a great deal to say about drunkenness:

*For the drunkard and the glutton shall come to poverty: and drowsiness shall clothe a man with rags.*
(Proverbs 23:31, KJV)

*Blessed art thou, O land, when thy king is the son of nobles, and thy princes eat in due season, for strength, and not for drunkenness!*
(Ecclesiastes 10:17, KJV)

*The earth shall reel to and fro like a drunkard, and shall be removed like a cottage; and the transgression thereof shall*

*be heavy upon it; and it shall fall, and not rise again.*
(Isaiah 24:20, KJV)

*Awake, ye drunkards, and weep; and howl, all ye drinkers of wine, because of the new wine; for it is cut off from your mouth.*
(Joel 1:5, KJV)

*Let us walk honestly, as in the day; not in rioting and drunkenness, not in chambering and wantonness, not in strife and envying.*
(Romans 13:13, KJV)

*Nor thieves, nor covetous, nor drunkards, nor revilers, nor extortioners, shall inherit the kingdom of God.*
(1 Corinthians 6:10, KJV)

*And be not drunk with wine, wherein is excess; but be filled with the Spirit.*
(Ephesians 5:18, KJV)

*With whom the kings of the earth have committed fornication, and the inhabitants of the earth have been made drunk with the wine of her fornication.*
(Revelation 17:2, KJV)

While there is no question that people did not have the variety of beverage choices we have today and that wine was a necessary part of ancient culture, it's also not of question that some people had difficulty maintaining balance and good sense when it came to consumption of alcohol. Xerxes was one of them, at least at this point in his life, because alcohol signified social interaction, good times, wealth and liberality, and all those things that go along with the desire to take those initial drinks so many do. Xerxes proves to us that alcohol indulgence leads to alcohol problems, and that with that slippery slope comes decisions that compromise and impact on the lives of others.

Xerxes also proves another fact we often gloss over in the Scriptures: not all men in the Bible are perfect or angelic in their nature. We are quick to vilify women who do the wrong thing in Scripture, but we ignore the things that men do that are less than ideal. Moses got angry, Noah got drunk, David got in bed with someone he shouldn't have, Gideon made God prove himself an awful lot, Solomon had a wandering eye for too many women, and Xerxes was, at this point in his life, a drunken mess. These parts of the story are there for us and our learning, to see that God's plan outweighs the messiest parts of our existence. Behind that we also learn that even the best can fall awry and even the worst can change. Faith isn't often as clean-cut as we'd hope it will be. By sanitizing Bible characters, we are overlooking the message that lies in their messiness. If we embrace their mess, we can see through our own unto the divine hope and promise of change.

**Esther 1:9-18**

**Queen Vashti also gave a banquet for the women in the royal palace of King Xerxes.**
**On the seventh day, when King Xerxes was in high spirits from wine, he commanded the seven eunuchs who served him - Mehuman, Biztha, Harbona, Bigtha, Abagtha, Zethar and Carcas - to bring before him Queen Vashti, wearing her royal crown, in order to display her beauty to the people and nobles, for she was lovely to look at. But when the attendants delivered the king's command, Queen Vashti refused to come. Then the king became furious and burned with anger.**
**Since it was customary for the king to consult experts in matters of law and justice, he spoke with the wise men who understood the times and were closest to the king - Carshena, Shethar, Admatha, Tarshish, Meres, Marsena and Memucan, the seven nobles of Persia and Media who had special access to the king and were highest in the kingdom.**

*"According to the law, what must be done to Queen Vashti?" he asked. "She has not obeyed the command of King Xerxes that the eunuchs have taken to her."*

*The Memucan replied in the presence of the king and the nobles, "Queen Vashti has done wrong, not only against the king but also against all the nobles and the peoples of all the provinces of King Xerxes. For the queen's conduct will become known to all the women, and so they will despise their husbands and say, 'King Xerxes commanded Queen Vashti to be brought before him, but she would not come.' This very day, the Persian and Median women of the nobility who have heard about the queen's conduct will respond to all the king's nobles in the same way. There will be no end of disrespect and discord.*

(Related Bible references: Proverbs 19:12, Proverbs 20:2, Matthew 3:1-12, Mark 6:14-29, Ephesians 5:18)

Vashti, wife of Xerxes, doesn't enter the picture until verse 9. Surprisingly enough, for all we hear about Queen Vashti, the Bible does not support a negative or rebellious view of her. As queen, it would have been her responsibility to hold a party for the women, as men and women were customarily set to different establishments and spheres in this part of the world, even in these times. The issues existing between men and women in the Middle East have a long history, even prior to the rise of Islam, and are an ingrained part of life in that part of the world. The segregation of the sexes was seen as being for safety reasons as much as it was for social ones, and for one woman to be in the presence of a group of men would have raised questions about her reputation or work within a society. We don't see any visible example that Vashti was a bad queen or an improper queen, hesitant to do her work or the required duties that would have been part of her life as wife of Xerxes. The Bible indicates she did her job and was faithful to her role.

Yet it's very possible that Vashti grew weary and tired of

Xerxes' endless partying, as for six months, without end, she was subject to his drunken self-glory and self-praise, having to reinforce how great he was and keep it together in public, lauding and smiling as the experience wore on. The tired encounters with a drunk man who kept calling for her and wanting her to lavish attention on him in his drunken state wore old and boring, yet Vashti still persevered on, even though she might have grown tired of it. Vashti lived with the situation so many wives of addicts also deal with: the constant need to bolster and cover up their inadequacies and overlook their belittling and negative behavior...until she just couldn't take any more of it.

In his drunken state, full of himself and of his alcoholic haze, Xerxes called for his servants to go and bring Queen Vashti to him, wearing her royal crown (and as the original languages indicate, not much else), to parade and dance in her splendor before his men. She was to wear the crown to prove she was his property, displaying herself as belonging to him. We went from celebrating the nations and the conquests of Persia to now a far more personal celebration, one that treated Vashti as if she was common property, as exclusively his, to do and demand for whatever purpose he wanted, at any time.

Vashti had but one choice: it was the one that upheld her dignity and self-respect and risked her very life. That choice was to refuse to go and present herself before Xerxes and his men. What he asked her to do could have endangered her well-being, left her as a victim of sexual assault, or something even more unimaginable and worse than these situations, and thus Vashti wasn't left an option to do anything else. It was her or him and given the past six months had been all about him, Vashti had enough, and she refused to present herself at Xerxes' request.

The question, however, remains: what made Vashti say no? What made this woman, who had compromised for ages, do the right thing - and follow her instincts to say no? Vashti followed her own instincts that this wasn't right or safe for her, and she did what she knew she had to do, following the leading of a God that she did not know, nor worship. Much like Ruth followed her instincts to go with Naomi to Bethlehem, and Esther followed instincts as to her actions and placement within the Persian kingdom, so Vashti followed her instincts, which were God-given and God-led, unto the end of risking it all for her self-respect and dignity.

For this reason, Vashti finds herself on the list of controversial female Biblical figures. Vashti has come to represent a certain independent identity and spirit that we do not encourage, nor laud, nor educate, in women. Women are encouraged to assimilate their identities into their birth families, then their husbands, and then their nuclear families, always and in all things yielding to male desire and identity. Yet when a woman constantly yields to male authority and it costs her something – whether it is virginity or sexual status, attire, co-dependency, or personal demoralization – we condemn women for yielding to that state of assimilation, of surrendering power, or giving up personal identity. We shame her, telling her she should have known better or done something different, that whatever happened was her fault, and that she brought it on herself. We commonly call this "victim shaming," and the way we view Vashti proves it isn't a new phenomenon in our world. When women are shamed regardless of what they do, that tells us something about a societal disregard for women. Vashti's actions were so revolutionary, she received public condemnation of those in her day, and even to the present day, of preachers, scholars, and other women, who find her self-respect and interest as scandalous, rather than an icon of what we should all aspire to do when we are in situations that violate our self-worth and self-respect. Vashti teaches us all that we are more valuable than abuse, and that no matter what anyone might want to preserve in church, abuse in any form – emotional, financial, physical, sexual, verbal, and mental – is not all right, hearing such cry out to us by the inward witness of God.

*In those days there appeared John the Baptist, preaching in the Wilderness (Desert) of Judea*

And saying, Repent (think differently; change your mind, regretting your sins and changing your conduct), for the kingdom of heaven is at hand.

This is he who was mentioned by the prophet Isaiah when he said, The voice of one crying in the wilderness (shouting in the desert), Prepare the road for the Lord, make His highways straight (level, direct).

This same John's garments were made of camel's hair, and he wore a leather girdle about his waist; and his food was locusts and wild honey.

Then Jerusalem and all Judea and all the country round about the Jordan went out to him;

And they were baptized in the Jordan by him, confessing their sins.

But when he saw many of the Pharisees and Sadducees coming for baptism, he said to them, You brood of vipers! Who warned you to flee and escape from the wrath and indignation [of God against disobedience] that is coming?

Bring forth fruit that is consistent with repentance [let your lives prove your change of heart];

And do not presume to say to yourselves, We have Abraham for our forefather; for I tell you, God is able to raise up descendants for Abraham from these stones!

And already the ax is lying at the root of the trees; every tree therefore that does not bear good fruit is cut down and thrown into the fire.

I indeed baptize you in (with) water because of repentance [that is, because of your changing your minds for the better, heartily amending your ways, with abhorrence of your past *sins]. But He Who is coming after me is mightier than I, Whose sandals I am not worthy or fit to take off or carry; He will baptize you with the Holy Spirit and with fire.*

*His winnowing fan (shovel, fork) is in His hand, and He will thoroughly clear out and clean His threshing floor and gather and store His wheat in His barn, but the chaff He will burn up with fire that cannot be put out.*
(Matthew 3:1-12, AMPC)

*I tell you the truth, John the Baptist is greater than any other person ever born [born to women], but even the least important person in the kingdom of heaven is greater than John [because John prepares for, but does not fully participate in the blessings of the kingdom]. Since the time [From the days] John the Baptist came until now, the kingdom of heaven has been going forward in strength [advancing forcefully; or subject to violence; suffering violent attacks], and forceful [or violent] people have been trying to take it by force [lay hold of it; or attack it]. All the prophets and the law of Moses told about what would happen [prophesied] until the time John came [John]. And if you will believe what they said, you will believe that John is Elijah [are willing to accept it, he is Elijah], whom they said would come. Let those with ears use them and listen [The one who has ears to hear, let him hear]!*
(Matthew 11:11-15, EXB)

*And king Herod heard of him; (for his name was spread abroad:) and he said, That John the Baptist was risen from the dead, and therefore mighty works do shew forth themselves in him.*

*Others said, That it is Elias. And others said, That it is a prophet, or as one of the prophets.*

*But when Herod heard thereof, he said, It is John, whom I beheaded: he is risen from the dead.*

*For Herod himself had sent forth and laid hold upon John, and bound him in prison for Herodias' sake, his brother Philip's wife: for he had married her.*

*For John had said unto Herod, It is not lawful for thee to have thy brother's wife.*

*Therefore Herodias had a quarrel against him, and would have killed him; but she could not:*

*For Herod feared John, knowing that he was a just man and an holy, and observed him; and when he heard him, he did many things, and heard him gladly.*

*And when a convenient day was come, that Herod on his birthday made a supper to his lords, high captains, and chief estates of Galilee;*

*And when the daughter of the said Herodias came in, and danced, and pleased Herod and them that sat with him, the king said unto the damsel, Ask of me whatsoever thou wilt, and I will give it thee.*

*And he sware unto her, Whatsoever thou shalt ask of me, I will give it thee, unto the half of my kingdom.*

*And she went forth, and said unto her mother, What shall I ask? And she said, The head of John the Baptist.*

*And she came in straightway with haste unto the king, and asked, saying, I will that thou give me by and by in a charger the head of John the Baptist.*

*And the king was exceeding sorry; yet for his oath's sake, and for their sakes which sat with him, he would not reject her.*

*And immediately the king sent an executioner, and commanded his head to be brought: and he went and beheaded him in the prison,*

*And brought his head in a charger, and gave it to the damsel: and the damsel gave it to her mother.*

*And when his disciples heard of it, they came and took up his corpse, and laid it in a tomb.*
(Mark 6:14-29, KJV)

The stand that Vashti made was so unconventional and unheard of for her time, she challenged every power that was in her day. Her wild nature, one that called her out into the wilderness from her position within society, turned her into a rebel, into a type of John the Baptist, the one who went before Jesus Christ to make the way for Him. Vashti stepped out to be different, punished for doing the right thing, and challenged the establishment, all in the process. John, too was different, was punished for doing what was right, and challenged the establishment, all just by doing what he was supposed to do. Thus, for Esther to enter the picture, Vashti first had to make the way – and she did so, by going out of the kingdom empire of the world and into the wilderness, to come deeper into God's Kingdom, all part of God's unique purpose in what was to come.

    Yet Xerxes didn't get his way, and because he was acting like a heathen without any foresight to the future, he had a way of making sure he got whatever he wanted out of the situation. He was mad and called his consultants in the law to figure out just what to do to Vashti. They were afraid that as Vashti was seen as a role model, the women of the provinces would also start to gain a sense of courage and self-respect and start disobeying their husbands in things they shouldn't be doing. From marriage, to ministry, to the workplace, to friendships, and to a host of other things we see in this world, people claim to want us, but in a specific context, and when they are refused on the grounds of our personal morality, we find ourselves all too often as Vashti: they are afraid we might influence others, and that means we suddenly – and quickly, have to depart the kingdom.

## Esther 1:19-22

*"Therefore, if it pleases the king, let him issue a royal decree and let it be written in the laws of Persia and Media, which cannot be repealed, that Vashti is never again to enter the presence of King Xerxes. Also let the king give her royal position to someone else who is better than she. Then when the king's edict is proclaimed throughout all his vast realm, all the women will respect their husbands, from the least to the greatest."*

*The king and his nobles were pleased with this advice, so the king did as Memucan proposed. He sent dispatches to all parts of the kingdom, to each province in its own script and to each people in its own language, proclaiming in each people's tongue that every man should be ruler over his own household.*

(Related Bible references: Daniel 6:8, Daniel 6:15)

Thanks to Vashti, an entire law was written in response to the fear of God she shook up in these immoral and violating leaders. This wasn't just any law, however. The wording of the original Hebrew texts indicates men were to be more than just respected. The edict demands that men were to be treated as princes and rulers, and their wives were to pay homage to them as such, rather than just mere husbands. It elevated men everywhere to royal status, leading to a sense of idolatry, and that women were to place their husbands and their desires above everything else in their lives. This tells us much of what he was looking for from Vashti between the lines: he wanted everyone to know that she belonged to him, and to do this action as a sign of putting him before anyone and anything else in her life, including her personal well-being and any understanding of a spiritual being. He wanted to be her god, and when she refused, he, like a jealous, angry idol, used every ounce of authority he had against her. She was banished from Xerxes' presence, she was criticized in her character as not being "good enough," all the work she had done was condemned, and it was declared that now that she'd made the way, someone else – Esther – could enter the picture. She was free, but she paid a price for her freedom. Everyone was informed that Vashti was deposed, and the situation waited and resumed when the time would surface again, for another heroine to enter the picture. Yet we often talk of the courage of Esther, but it is just as relevant – and important – for us to talk about the courage of Vashti. Esther's story didn't start with her ascent to the throne, but with a woman who'd had enough and dared to walk away from alcoholism, spousal mistreatment, and fear into something unknown, a hero unto herself listening to the voice of God, who was truly brave in her conduct and decision.

# CHAPTER SIX
Laying Foundations in the Midst of a Conspiracy
(Esther Chapter 2)

### Key verses

- **Verses 2-4:** Then the king's personal attendants proposed, "let a search be made for beautiful young virgins for the king. Let the king appoint commissioners in every province of his realm to bring all these beautiful girls into the harem at the citadel of Susa. Let them be placed under the care of Hegai, the king's eunuch, who is in charge of the women; and let beauty treatments be given to them. Then let the girl who pleases the king be queen instead of Vashti." This advice appealed to the king, and he followed it.

- **Verses 7-9:** Mordecai had a cousin named Hadassah, whom he had brought up because she had neither father nor mother. This girl, who was also known as Esther, was lovely in form and features, and Mordecai had taken her as his own daughter when her father and mother died. When the king's order and edict had been proclaimed, many girls were brought to the citadel of Susa and put under the care of Hegai. Esther also was taken to the king's palace and entrusted to Hegai, who had charge of the harem. The girl pleased him and won his favor. Immediately he provided her with beauty treatments and special food. He assigned to her seven maids selected from the king's palace and moved her and her maids into the best place in the harem.

- **Verses 17-18:** Now the king was attracted to Esther more than to any of the other women, and she won his favor and approval more than any of the other virgins. So he set a royal crown on her head and made her queen instead of Vashti. And the king gave a great banquet, Esther's banquet, for all his nobles and officials. He proclaimed a holiday throughout the provinces and distributed gifts with royal liberality.

## Words and phrases to know

- **Later:** From the Hebrew word *'achar* which means "after the following part, behind (of place), hinder, afterwards (of time)."[1]

- **Harem:** From two Hebrew words: *bayith* which means "house; place; receptacle; home, house as containing a family; household, household affairs; inwards (metaph.); temple; on the inside prep; within"[2] and *'ishshah* which means "woman, wife, female."[3]

- **Hegai:** From the Hebrew word *Hege'* or *Hegay* which means "Hegai or Hege = 'eunuch;' one of the eunuchs of the court of Ahasuerus."[4]

- **Beauty Treatments:** From the Hebrew word *tamruwq* or *tamruq* which means "a scraping, rubbing; remedy (for an injury)."[5]

- **Pleases:** From the Hebrew word *yatab* which means "to be good, be pleasing, be well, be glad."[6]

- **Mordecai:** From the Hebrew word *Mordekay* which means "Mordecai = 'little man' or 'worshipper of Mars;' cousin and adoptive father of queen Esther; son of Jair of the tribe of Benjamin; deliverer under Divine providence of the children of Israel from the destruction plotted by Haman the chief minister of Ahasuerus; institutor of the feast of Purim; a Jew who returned from exile with Zerubbabel."[7]

- **Exile:** From the Hebrew word *galah* which means "to uncover, remove."[8]

- **Nebuchadnezzar:** From the Hebrew word *Nebuwkadne'tstsar*, *Nebukadne'tstsar* (2 Ki 24:1, 10), or *Nebuwkadnetstsar* (Est 2:6, Dan 1:18), *Nebuwkadre'tstsar* or *Nebuwkadre'tstsowr* (Ez 2:1, Jer 49:28) which means "Nebuchadnezzar or Nebuchadrezzar = 'may Nebo protect the crown;; the great king of Babylon who captured Jerusalem and carried Judah captive."[9]

- **Jehoiachin:** From the Hebrew word *Yekonyah* and *Yekonyahuw* or (Jer 27:20) *Yekowneyah* which means "Jeconiah = 'Jehovah will establish;' son of king Jehoiakim of Judah and king of Judah for 3 months and 10 days before he surrendered to Nebuchadnezzar and was taken captive to Babylon where he was imprisoned for the next 36 years; released at the death of Nebuchadnezzar and lived in Babylon until his death."[10]

- **Hadassah:** From the Hebrew word *Hadaccah* which means "Hadassah = 'myrtle;' Queen Esther's Jewish name."[11]

- **Esther:** From the Hebrew word *'Ecter* which means "Esther = 'star;' the queen of Persia, heroine of the book of Esther - daughter of Abihail, cousin and adopted daughter of Mordecai, of the tribe of Benjamin, made queen by king Ahasuerus to replace divorced queen, Vashti.[12]

- **Shaashgaz:** From the Hebrew word *Sha`ashgaz* which means "Shaashgaz = 'servant of the beautiful;' the eunuch in the palace of Xerxes who was in charge of the women in the 2nd house."[13]

- **Concubines:** From the Hebrew word *piylegesh* or *pilegesh* which means "concubine, paramour."[14]

- **Summoned:** From the Hebrew word *qara'* which means "to call, call out, recite, read, cry out, proclaim."[15]

- **Adopted:** From two Hebrew words: *laqach* which means "to take, get, fetch, lay hold of, seize, receive, acquire, buy, bring, marry, take a wife, snatch, take away"[16] and *bath* which means "daughter, girl, adopted daughter, daughter-in-law, sister, granddaughters, female child, cousin."[17]

- **Attracted:** From the Hebrew word *'ahab* or *'aheb* which means "to love, human love for another, includes family, and sexual, human appetite for objects such as food, drink, sleep, wisdom, human love for or to God, act of being a friend, lover (participle), friend, God's love toward man, to individual men, to people Israel, to righteousness, lovely, loveable, friends, lovers (fig. of adulterers); to like."[18]

- **Bigthana:** From the Hebrew word *Bigthan* or *Bigthana'* which means "Bigthan = 'in their wine-press;' a eunuch in king Ahasuerus' (Xerxes) court.[19]

- **Teresh:** From the Hebrew word *Teresh* which means "Teresh = 'strictness;' one of the 2 eunuchs who plotted to kill king Ahasuerus of Persia but whose plot was discovered by Mordecai."[20]

- **Gallows:** From the Hebrew word `ets which means "tree, wood, timber, stock, plank, stalk, stick, gallows."[21]

- **Book of the annals:** From two Hebrew words: *cepher* which means "book"[22] and *dabar* which means "speech, word, speaking, thing."[23]

## Esther 2:1-4

**Later when the anger of King Xerxes had subsided, he remembered Vashti and what she had done and what he had decreed about her. Then the king's personal attendants proposed, "Let a search be made for beautiful young virgins for the king. Let the king appoint commissioners in every province of his realm to bring all these beautiful girls into the harem at the citadel of Susa. Let them be placed under the care of Hegai, the king's eunuch, who is in charge of the women; and let beauty treatments be given to them. Then let the girl who pleases the king be queen instead of Vashti." This advice appealed to the king, and he followed it.**

(Related Bible references: Proverbs 16:18, Matthew 19:10-12, Romans 8:28-31)

Sometimes when we read the Scriptures, we tend to think chapters and verses pass from one day to the next. In between some passages, there are more than days or weeks; there can be years. Where Esther 1 leaves off and Esther 2 picks up gaps a period of four years. It is believed Xerxes was off in this period trying to conquer Greece, which was a failure. It's not a big leap to realize that such a massive endeavor changes someone, and I believe it, to a certain extent, changed Xerxes, as well. While the book of Esther begins with a proud Xerxes who was known for military seizure and conquest, Greece was too much for Xerxes to take. Sometimes it takes our failures to humble us, and as much as we dislike failure, sometimes it brings us to exactly where we need to be. To say God only uses promotion, and not personal failures, is a misnomer of Bible experience and context. If we understand the Scriptures properly, God uses everything - the good and the bad - to bring us to a realization of Him and of ourselves in our lives.

*Pride goes before destruction, and a haughty spirit before a fall.*
(Proverbs 16:18, ESV)

*We are assured and know that [God being a partner in their labor] all things work together and are [fitting into a plan] for good to and for those who love God and are called according to [His] design and purpose.*

*For those whom He foreknew [of whom He was aware and loved beforehand], He also destined from the beginning [foreordaining them] to be molded into the image of His Son [and share inwardly His likeness], that He might become the firstborn among many brethren.*

*And those whom He thus foreordained, He also called; and those whom He called, He also justified (acquitted, made righteous, putting them into right standing with Himself). And those whom He justified, He also glorified [raising them to a heavenly dignity and condition or state of being].*

*What then shall we say to [all] this? If God is for us, who [can be] against us? [Who can be our foe, if God is on our side?]*
(Romans 8:28-31, AMPC)

Sometimes we must trust God in our falls. It's not so much

about immediately jumping up or becoming greater than we were before, but about learning to navigate what tripped up our fall in the first place. Xerxes might have been a mighty warrior and a powerful intimidator, but that doesn't mean he was all there when it came to right leadership or personal relationships. Xerxes' behavior in regards to his six-month long celebration of self and then his treatment of Vashti tells us much about him as a person, and all of it is undesirable. Xerxes was motivated and moved by pride, by self-love and admiration, and by personal amazement at his conquests. Vashti knew enough of herself to resist becoming yet another symbol in his long line of personal achievements. Many might say that Xerxes' fall didn't happen until he hit the battlefield, but his fall first started with Vashti's refusal to come and present herself as property. It marked the beginning of a period in his life where Xerxes would come to taste and know failure in an intimate and personal way, and that meant it would take him a while to process its taste and touch as it hit him in the face.

Xerxes would have to have a far softer perspective and a much greater desire to please another to marry Esther and favorably handle the requests she would bring before him. Vashti made Xerxes fall, bruising his pride and making the way for him to handle himself differently in intimate situations. Forever the way maker, Xerxes was angry with Vashti for years, working out his aggressions and hostilities as he nursed his bruised ego and hurt pride.

Whether or not we want to admit it, there's a little bit of Xerxes in all of us. We all want others to marvel over what we have and when our relationships come crashing down (for whatever their reason), we all nurse a bruised ego and wounded pride because we expected a different outcome. It's often the greatest internal desire we house: that others will envy what we have, believing that we are the most desirable of all people for our successful and long-lasting relationship. When that hope falls apart, we nurse the pain of lost hopes and dreams, and the frailty of our own personal egos on display for all. Successive losses lead us to desire to start something up with someone else right away, because that means we are the "victor" over our loss and heartache. And while I am a believer that love and successful relationships hit us when they come along (and that we should never take such for granted or brush off what might come quickly and swiftly to us), we also shouldn't be out looking for a relationship during a period of our lives that should be reserved for healing, recovery, and developing a new outlook. With all his power and influence, Xerxes could have looked for a wife the day after Vashti was banished from the kingdom, but that wasn't his choice. It wouldn't have been right, and it would have been outside of the proper timing. Giving heed to this reminds all of us that relationships don't heal easily, and we can be angry about situations from them months to years after they are over.

When the time was right, Xerxes was advised to start looking for a new queen. The commissioners of all the provinces were to conduct searches for eligible, young virginal women who would then be brought to the harem present at Susa. We often depict harems as locations for licentious, sexual prostitution games, but a harem is simply a dwelling place or portion of a large house that is specifically for the women. The existence of a harem gives us greater detail into the lives of Persian women and Persian settings, in some ways down to the present day. In gender-segregated societies, men and women have both respective dwellings and societal placements, and these codes of conduct were a large part of life for women, such as Esther.

We also see the introduction of such characters as Hegai, who was the eunuch in charge of the women in the harem. Eunuchs were also a large part of ancient royal societies, often with no rights or dignities of their own. The literal definition of a eunuch is a male individual who was castrated (removal of the testicles) prior to the onset of puberty. Such a procedure probably sounds horrifying by modern standards, but it wasn't uncommon in ancient times. It was often done without the male's consent; deliberately done to prepare them for the work of service they would fulfil. It was believed that by castrating men they would become trustworthy with women, and more loyal to their masters. Though classified as servants (and often having slave status), eunuchs were trusted officials and positioned to care for women in harems in these sexually segregated societies.[24]

The term "eunuch" grew to include men who might have served in the traditional role of a castrated male (especially caring for the women) but was not, in fact, physically castrated. It was likely a term for a male who, being trustworthy with women, was understood to have no attraction to them (such as in the case of a homosexual male) or a male who, for some other reason, was unable to marry or unable to procreate.[25] It also, by extension, would reference individuals we might classify as transgender today, crossing gender boundaries in dress and attire by virtue of their ambiguous gender.

The inclusion of Hegai by name in this particular passage of Scripture opens the door wide for three groups of people (as well as the inclusion of other very respected eunuchs later in Esther): those whose situations are not typical and do not fall into what one might consider the "norm," those who are non-procreative for whatever the reason may be, and those who assist and build up in ways that we frequently don't consider. Hegai is mentioned in this passage without any reference or frame of understanding. We know nothing about his life, and there's no way to spin off an entire story about him alone, based on this information. He was a trusted servant of the king, serving in the role of a eunuch within the palace. Yet he wasn't a typical man, by virtue of his work and by the posture either imposed upon him or within him from birth. Still, typical or not, he was present at this time to touch destiny, for a specific purpose in a specific time, and do what he was appointed to do.

*His disciples say unto Him, If the case of the man be so with his wife, it is not good to marry.*

*But He said unto them, All men cannot receive this saying, save they to whom it is given.*

*For there are some eunuchs, which were so born from their mother's womb: and there are some eunuchs, which were made eunuchs of men: and there be eunuchs, which have made themselves eunuchs for the kingdom of heaven's sake. He that is able to receive it, let him receive it.*
(Matthew 19:10-12, KJV)

Hegai was a part of this Kingdom promise, a part of this destiny to stand as different and unique for a spiritual purpose that he, most likely, didn't understand. No matter how he became a eunuch, he was there by God's purpose. Sincere and responsible, he understood about the women and their daily activities, their beauty treatments, and, most relevantly, deciding who would be suitable as the next queen of the Persian Empire.

We need to be more open (especially as believers, and most definitely as the church) to receive help and assistance from others who might, in some way, be different than we are. If there is one thing we can clearly see, it is that it took many different and diverse abilities, callings, stations, and yes, even different orientations or identities to make an empire work. As Christians, our diversity of life should reflect in those who assist in building our work. Anyone can provide a word from God at any time, no matter who they are or what one might think of them, and we should be open to the different ways God desires to speak and reach out to us. You never know just who God desires to use to impact or bless your life, and you never know who He desires for you to impact by letting someone touch yours.

## Esther 2:5-18

**Now there was in the citadel of Susa a Jew of the tribe of Benjamin, named Mordecai son of Jair, the son of Shimei, the son of Kish, who had been carried into exile from**

Jerusalem by Nebuchadnezzar king of Babylon, among those taken captive with Jehoiachin king of Judah. Mordecai had a cousin named Hadassah, whom he had brought up because she had neither father nor mother. This girl, who was also known as Esther, was lovely in form and features, and Mordecai had taken her as his own daughter when her father and mother died.

When the king's order and edict had been proclaimed, many girls were brought to the citadel of Susa and put under the care of Hegai. Esther also was taken to the king's palace and entrusted to Hegai, who had charge of the harem. The girl pleased him and won his favor. Immediately he provided her with beauty treatments and special food. He assigned to her seven maids selected from the king's palace and moved her and her maids into the best place in the harem.

Esther had not revealed her nationality and family background, because Mordecai had forbidden her to do so. Every day he walked back and forth near the courtyard of the harem to find out how Esther was and what was happening to her.

Before a girl's turn came to go in to King Xerxes, she had to complete twelve months of beauty treatments prescribed for the women, six months with oil of myrrh and six with perfume and cosmetics. And this is how she would go to the king: Anything she wanted was given her to take with her from the harem to the king's palace. In the evening she would go there and in the morning return to another part of the harem to the care of Shaashgaz, the king's eunuch who was in charge of the concubines. She would not return to the king unless he was pleased with her and summoned her by name.

When the turn came for Esther (the girl Mordecai had adopted, the daughter of his uncle Abihail) to go to the king, she asked for nothing other than what Hegai, the king's eunuch who was in charge of the harem, suggested. And Esther won the favor of everyone who saw her. She was taken to King Xerxes in the royal *residence in the tenth month, the month of Tebeth, in the seventh year of his reign.*

***Now the king was attracted to Esther more than to any of the other women, and she won his favor and approval more than any of the other virgins. So he set a royal crown on her head and made her queen instead of Vashti. And the king gave a great banquet, Esther's banquet, for all his nobles and officials. He proclaimed a holiday throughout the provinces and distributed gifts with royal liberality.***

(Related Bible references: Genesis 3:15, Genesis 49:27, 2 Kings 24:14-15, Jeremiah 22:28, Jeremiah 24:1, Jeremiah 37:1, Jeremiah 52:31, Matthew 1:11, Galatians 5:22-23, Hebrews 6:20-7:8, James 1:27)

Now the story shifts to how all these different entities will come together to change history. First in is Mordecai (name means "little man" or "worshiper of Mars" which implies being a warrior or aggressive individual), the son of Jair (name means "he shines") a Benjamite, and cousin to a young woman named Hadassah (name means "myrtle tree"), also named Esther (name means "star" in Persian), who he adopted as his own daughter when her parents died. Mordecai's name tells us much about him: he was a warrior, whether it was in a military sense we do not know, but we can tell he was a spiritual warrior, one who knew how to be strategic and relevant in every situation. Mordecai knew how to keep his ear to the ground and how to rise up when necessary, and how to handle each situation that came along. Familiar with life outside of Israel or Judah, Mordecai was the second generation of his family born outside of his ancestral land.

Mordecai's cousin, Esther, is the one who enters the picture to stand as a savior for her people by following his strategy and leadership. Of everyone in the book of Esther, we know the most about Esther and her background. Positioned for great purpose, Esther was orphaned at a young age and lived without a father or mother. While in modern times this can echo a superhero-like status, it should also reiterate for us a powerful building block as Esther begins to unveil for us her type as a type of Christ Himself, echoing the tradition of the priesthood of Melchizedek.

*After his [Abram's] return from the defeat and slaying of Chedorlaomer and the kings who were with him, the king of Sodom went out to meet him at the Valley of Shaveh, that is, the King's Valley.*

*Melchizedek king of Salem [later called Jerusalem] brought out bread and wine [for their nourishment]; he was the priest of God Most High,*

*And he blessed him and said, Blessed (favored with blessings, made blissful, joyful) be Abram by God Most High, Possessor and Maker of heaven and earth,*

*And blessed, praised, and glorified be God Most High, Who has given your foes into your hand! And [Abram] gave him a tenth of all [he had taken].*
(Genesis 14:17-20, AMPC)

*Where Jesus has entered in for us [in advance], a Forerunner having become a High Priest forever after the order (with the rank) of Melchizedek.*

*For this Melchizedek, king of Salem [and] priest of the Most High God, met Abraham as he returned from the slaughter of the kings and blessed him,*

*And Abraham gave to him a tenth portion of all [the spoil]. He is primarily, as his name when translated indicates, king of righteousness, and then he is also king of Salem, which means king of peace.*

*Without [record of] father or mother or ancestral line, neither with beginning of days nor ending of life, but, resembling the*

*Son of God, he continues to be a priest without interruption and without successor.*

*Now observe and consider how great [a personage] this was to whom even Abraham the patriarch gave a tenth [the topmost or the pick of the heap] of the spoils.*

*And it is true that those descendants of Levi who are charged with the priestly office are commanded in the Law to take tithes from the people—which means, from their brethren—though these have descended from Abraham.*

*But this person who has not their Levitical ancestry received tithes from Abraham [himself] and blessed him who possessed the promises [of God].*

*Yet it is beyond all contradiction that it is the lesser person who is blessed by the greater one.*

*Furthermore, here [in the Levitical priesthood] tithes are received by men who are subject to death; while there [in the case of Melchizedek], they are received by one of whom it is testified that he lives [perpetually].*
(Hebrews 6:20-7:8, AMPC)

Jesus was associated with Melchizedek, King of Salem because his title related to being the "king of peace," but also because Melchizedek represented a spiritual priesthood, one that did not have a beginning nor an ending, as we have no history nor lineage for the life of Melchizedek. He is a figure that seems to enter the Scriptures from nowhere, has an exchange with Abraham, receives Abraham's tithes, and blesses him. He does not appear to have a father or a mother, and did something that eternally impacted subsequent generations of faith. Likewise, Esther seemingly appears of nowhere, in the nation of Persia, with no claim to fame and no real identity, as she was adopted by her cousin. Like Melchizedek, Esther has no father or mother, and she is put in a position to be received by those among her who do not share her faith. A light shining in a dark place, Esther's role as a type of Christ begins with her identity as one without a traditional family.

Biblically speaking, we pay great attention to male types of Christ. We love to look out and see Christ's typology in men such as Moses or David, but we forget that types do not have to be gender-bound to be authentic. Just as Moses' temper was not a prefigure of Christ's nature and David's adultery had nothing to do with anything Jesus would ever do, gender is not a precursor to authentic typology. If Vashti was a type of John the Baptist, then Esther was a type of Christ, just as John paved the way for Jesus. Just as Jesus did, Esther displayed a victory over the enemy, bringing life and hope to the situation her people found themselves, in, and stood ready to overcome as was in the garden in Genesis 3:15:

*I will make you and the woman*
   *enemies to each other [place hostility/enmity between you and the woman].*
*Your descendants [seed] and her descendants [seed]*
   *will be enemies.*
*One of her descendants [He] will crush your head,*
   *and you will bite [strike; bruise; crush] His heel [Rom. 16:20; Rev. 12:9]. (EXB)*

As a woman of Jewish lineage, Esther assumed a royal position. Here in Esther, and in the work of Vashti as well, we see this visual enmity between Satan's work and these women, who were appointed and positioned to take stands against the social and spiritual evils of their day. This promise and this prophecy is why this work was handed over to women; it is why the book is called Esther, not Edward, or Earnest, or Eric, or the name of some other male figure in history. Esther displayed a victory over the enemy using skill and purpose and being willing to make the ultimate sacrifice for her own people. The woman had the victory over the enemy; only as she was willing to be divinely led and crush his head.

As many other young women, Esther found herself in the citadel of Susa under Hegai's care. She was favored by him for her countenance. Here, in the midst of this place, Esther's collaborations - both with her non-parental relative and a queer character, and eunuch charted with her care - she finds favor. Staring around her there were dozens of other young, attractive girls who could have easily seen her as a competing force, or she see them as the same. Yet Esther teaches us something important about our character and our character when it comes to issues of beauty and personal interaction with others. It's very true that it's possible to be the most beautiful person in the room, but also the ugliest because of how we interact in our behavior. Esther stood out among the other young women with her character, which was pleasant. In the face of an unknown situation that could have easily generated fear or a feeling of real threat, Esther responded with courage and pleasantness, treating others well and respecting the authority that was in place. Esther's character teaches us much about dealing with adversity and being in places where we might not always feel the most welcome or respond very well: we should never let such a circumstance change who we are called to be in our spiritual countenance, nor should we focus on physical attributes as much as we focus on personal character.

*But the Spirit produces the fruit of [fruit of the Spirit is] love, joy, peace, patience, kindness, goodness, faithfulness [or faith], gentleness, self-control. There is no law that says these things are wrong [or No law can oppose such things].* (Galatians 5:22-23, EXB)

If we conduct ourselves properly, there is no law, anywhere in the world, that will impede our interactions with others. Proper conduct, extending honor to others, respecting others are all universal messages that can reach individuals regardless of culture. They are a part of our witness to the world, and they are all part of how we experience the position and purpose of favor in our lives. She saw herself receive the best food, the best place in the harem, and seven maids (a number indicating perfection, marking her as notable and a viable candidate for queen) standing out from the rest. Esther didn't just receive favor because it was a part of a greater plan (it was), but also because she behaved in a manner that blessed others and showed Hegai, someone who was, by all judgments, quite different from her, that she had the ability to conduct herself with grace and interact with anyone, no matter who they might have been.

A few years back, I started hearing the expression, "Favor ain't fair." I believe Esther's story proves the opposite: favor is the very definition of fair. It is the eternal leveler, the proof that no matter your social status or class, you can be positioned for a purpose, to experience something different and impact those around you, because God's character has infiltrated your soul, spirit, and very being. Favor is where spirituality and character meet and proves we cannot have one that transforms without the other. Favor isn't random; it is deliberate, and it comes about when we make sure that our purpose is God's business on a personal level. God's business becomes personal when we are willing to let the Word transform us, infiltrate us, and change us, to turn us into a person that can show honor to the lowest or the greatest, because we, too, understand how to be and live bound by that same principle of honor. Some of us don't see favor because we have not committed to live honorably, recognizing others and respecting the image of God at work in those around us. If we are willing to honor others as a part of creation, even if we don't like or agree with them, favor will find us.

Still, Esther kept her race, spirituality, and familial status secret, for fear such would impede her chances with King Xerxes. Mordecai stood by, watching over her and guarding her movements. He kept up with her, proving that even though Esther might not have had parents, she still had someone who cares about her. Mordecai is another Biblical figure who opens the door for us to embrace and raise up stepparents, foster parents, adoptive parents, mentors, and anyone who steps in to raise a child in the absence of a biological parent (or sometimes alongside with them). "Family" doesn't always fit the standard mold we seek, and Mordecai clearly stepped in and recognized Esther's destiny before she properly understood it herself. We do not have to seek out family in blood relatives, because Spirit is stronger than blood. God can send us the guidance, the support, and the encouragement we need, whether it is in the form of a blood relative, or not.

The beauty treatments these women went through were intense and took a total of one year: six months with oil of myrrh and six months of perfume and cosmetics. They were aptly prepared to walk in before the king, adorned and stunning, so he could make his full decision on who he sought best for the position of queen. Those women who were called to go before the king were allowed to take anything they wanted from the harem, and they would then go in to spend the night with the king. In the morning, the women would then return to the harem, this time under the watch of Shaashgaz, who was eunuch over the concubines. The young women would enter as potential queens and come out as concubines, thus awaiting to know if they would find the king's favor to be queen, yet again. If the king desired to see any of the women again, he would call for them, but they were not free to go before the king again if he did not call them.

This means Esther was positioned for status as a concubine if she was not made queen, and, most likely, while Xerxes decided as to whether Esther would be queen, she had concubinage status. The difference between a wife and a concubine was the situation surrounding her engagement: wives had dowries (or bridal prices) associated with them, while concubines did not. They were not free to come and go as they pleased, and as the property of the king, the competition for attention was heavy among these women. Esther was poised to live as a concubine if she hadn't ascended to become Queen of Persia, as she did not have family and we do not know of her financial status. By positioning Esther in the king's harem, Mordecai was ensuring Esther would have some sort of a future, one that could position her for a much better life than average society could provide. The amount of faith this took was incredible and unspeakable and shows us just how much Mordecai influenced Esther in her life of faith.

Esther triumphed above the others as she continued to stand on favor, treating people right and extending courtesy and respect. She didn't come in demanding, maintained humility, didn't ask for too much, and knew enough to take suggestions from those with clout, such as Hegai. After her treatments were completed, it was her turn to meet with King Xerxes. He was attracted to her, she was favored by him, and once he made his decision, he set a royal crown on her head, thus positioning her to stand as queen, replacing Vashti. Instead of throwing himself a banquet, Xerxes was moved to give a banquet in Esther's honor, providing gifts and declaring a holiday. Rather than seeking to prove her as his own, Xerxes honored her, showing her the respect and position that she'd extended to all while in the care of the harem.

### Esther 2:19-23

**When the virgins were assembled a second time, Mordecai was sitting at the king's gate. But Esther had kept secret her family background and nationality just as Mordecai had told her to do, for she continued to follow Mordecai's instructions as she had done when he was bringing her up.**

**During the time Mordecai was sitting at the king's gate, Bigthana and Teresh, two of the king's officers who guarded the doorway, became angry and conspired to assassinate King Xerxes. But Mordecai found out about the plot and told Queen Esther, who in turn reported it to the king, giving credit to Mordecai. And when the report**

***was investigated and found to be true, the two officials were hanged on a gallows. All this was recorded in the book of the annals in the presence of the king.***

(Related Bible references: Ecclesiastes 10:20)

We can see from the end of this chapter that Mordecai and Esther were poised to lay foundations for the future issues to come within the Persian Empire. Esther maintained her silence on her background, recognizing Mordecai hadn't ever led her astray. He knew there was a time and a place for everything, just as there is for us, even today. Sometimes it's not wise to air everything out for others to hear or embrace, and that we must make inroads and conduct ourselves wisely for the whole of our being to stand accepted in difficult places. It also raises the issue that Esther and Xerxes were also a mixed, interfaith marriage, much like Ruth and Mahlon and Ruth and Boaz were. Once again, the marriage served a purpose, enabling the promised Redeemer to enter the picture one day and liberate all who desire to be free from sin. Without Esther's marriage to Xerxes, the Jewish people would have never survived long enough to see Christ come into this world. These interfaith marriages teach us something about ourselves; about interacting with others in this world; and that God's purpose and power can be brought about in any situation, no matter how unconventional or difficult they may seem to be.

With his ear forever to the ground, Mordecai learns about a conspiracy to assassinate King Xerxes by two of his trusted officers, the guards of the doorway. Whether Bigthana and Teresh operated on their own or as part of a larger plan, we honestly don't know. All we know is Mordecai found out, he took the matter to Esther, and Esther notified Xerxes, giving the credit back to Mordecai. The two officials were executed, the matter was recorded, and Mordecai and Esther established themselves as loyal and credible to the crown. This would all become relevant later, as both individuals proved themselves and their honesty to one of the most powerful men in the ancient world.

# Chapter Seven
## Here For Such a Time as This
## (Esther Chapters 3-6)

### Key verses

- **Chapter 3 verses 3-6:** *Then the royal officials at the king's gate asked Mordecai, "Why do you disobey the king's command?" Day after day they spoke to him but he refused to comply. Therefore they told Haman about it to see whether Mordecai's behavior would be tolerated, for he had told them he was a Jew. When Haman saw that Mordecai would not kneel down or pay him honor, he was enraged. Yet having learned who Mordecai's people were, he scorned the idea of killing only Mordecai. Instead Haman looked for a way to destroy all Mordecai's people, the Jews, throughout the whole kingdom of Xerxes.*

- **Chapter 3 verses 12-13:** *Then on the thirteenth day of the first month the royal secretaries were summoned. They wrote out in the script of each province and in the language of each people all Haman's orders to the king's satraps, the governors of the various provinces and the nobles of the various peoples. These were written in the name of King Xerxes himself and sealed with his own ring. Dispatches were sent by couriers to all the king's* *provinces with the order to destroy, kill, and annihilate all the Jews – young and old, women and little children – on a single day, the thirteenth day of the twelfth month, the month of Adar, and to plunder their goods.*

- **Chapter 4 verses 1-3:** *When Mordecai learned of all that had been done, he tore his clothes, put on sackcloth and ashes, and went out into the city, wailing loudly and bitterly. But he went only as far as the king's gate, because no one clothed in sackcloth was allowed to enter it. In every province to which the edict and order of the king came, there was great mourning among the Jews, with fasting, weeping, and wailing. Many lay in sackcloth and ashes.*

- **Chapter 4 verses 9-15:** *Hathach went back and reported to Esther what Mordecai had said. Then she instructed him to say to Mordecai, "All the king's officials and the people of the royal provinces know that for any man or woman who approaches the king in the inner court without being summoned the king has but one law: that he be put to death. The only exception to this is for the king to extend the gold scepter to him and spare his life. But thirty days have passed since I was called to go to the king." When Esther's words were reported to Mordecai, he sent back this answer: "Do not think that because you are in the king's house you alone of all the Jews will escape. For if you remain silent at this time, relief and deliverance for the Jews will arise from another place, but you and your father's family will perish. And who knows but that you have come to royal position for such a time as this?" Then Esther sent this reply to Mordecai: "Go, gather together all the Jews who are in Susa, and fast for me. Do not eat or drink for three days, night or day. I and my maids will fast as you do.*

When this is done, I will go to the king, even though it is against the law. And if I perish, I perish."

- **Chapter 5 verses 3-5:** Then the king asked, "What is it, Queen Esther? What is your request? Even up to half the kingdom, it will be given you." "If it pleases the king," replied Esther, "let the king, together with Haman, come today to a banquet I have prepared for him." "Bring Haman at once," the King said, "so that we may do what Esther asks."

- **Chapter 5 verses 10-13:** Calling together his friends and Zeresh, his wife, Haman boasted to them about his vast wealth, his many sons, and all the ways the king had honored him and how he had elevated him above the other nobles and officials. "And that's not all," Haman added. "I'm the only person Queen Esther invited to accompany the king to the banquet she gave. And she has invited me along with the king tomorrow. But all this gives me no satisfaction as long as I see that Jew Mordecai sitting at the king's gate."

- **Chapter 6 verses 10-13:** "Go at once," the king commanded Haman. "Get the robe and the horse and do just as you have suggested for Mordecai the Jew, who sits at the king's gate. Do not neglect anything you have recommended." So Haman got the robe and the horse. He robed Mordecai, and led him on horseback through the city streets, proclaiming before him, "This is what is done for the man the king delights to honor!" Afterward Mordecai returned to the king's gate. But Haman rushed home, with his head covered in grief, and told Zeresh his wife and all his friends everything that had happened to him. His advisers and his wife Zeresh said to him, "Since Mordecai, before whom your downfall has started, is of Jewish origin, *you cannot stand against him – you will surely come to ruin!"*

## **Words and phrases to know**

- **Haman son of Hammedatha the Agagite:** From three Hebrew words: *Haman* which means "Haman = 'magnificent;' chief minister of Ahasuerus, enemy of Mordecai and the Jews, who plotted to kill the Jews but, being foiled by Esther, was hanged, with his family, on the gallows he had made for Mordecai;"[1] *Medatha* which means "Hammedatha = 'double'; father of Haman;"[2] and *'Agagiy* which means "Agagite = 'I will overtop;' said of Haman, Haman the Agagite."[3]

- **Kneel down:** From the Hebrew word *kara`* which means "to bend, kneel, bow, bow down, sink down to one's knees, kneel down to rest (of animals), kneel in reverence."[4]

- **Pur:** From the Hebrew word *Puwr* also *Puwriym* or *Puriym* which means "Pur or Purim = 'lot' or 'piece;' lot, a special feast among the post-exilic Jews, to celebrate their deliverance from Haman's destruction through queen Esther's heroic actions."[5]

- **Signet ring:** From the Hebrew word *tabba`ath* which means "ring, signet, signet ring."[6]

- **Satraps:** From the Hebrew word *'achashdarpan* which means "satrap, a governor of a Persian province."[7]

- **Annihiliate:** From the Hebrew word *'abad* which means "perish, vanish, go astray, be destroyed."[8]

- **Sackcloth:** From the Hebrew word *saq* which means "mesh, sackcloth, sack, sacking."[9]

- **Ashes:** From the Hebrew word *'epher* which means "ashes; worthlessness."[10]

- **King's gate:** From two Hebrew words: *melek* which means "king"[11] and *sha`ar* which means "gate."[12]

- **Fasting:** From the Hebrew word *tsowm* or *tsom* which means "fast, fasting."[13]

- **Weeping and wailing:** From two Hebrew words: *bekiy* which means "a weeping, weeping"[14] and *micepd* which means "wailing."[15]

- **Hathach:** From the Hebrew word *Hathak* which means "Hatach = 'verily;' a eunuch in the court of Ahasuerus."[16]

- **Deliverance:** From the Hebrew word *hatstsalah* which means "deliverance, escape."[17]

- **For such a time as this:** From the Hebrew word *`eth* which means "time, time (of an event), time (usual), experiences, fortunes, occurrence, occasion."[18]

- **Perish:** From the Hebrew word *'abad* which means "perish, vanish, go astray, be destroyed."[19]

- **Tip of the scepter:** From two Hebrew words: *ro'sh* which means "head, top, summit, upper part, chief, total, sum, height, front, beginning"[20] and *sharbiyt* which means "scepter; dart, spear."[21]

- **Zeresh:** From the Hebrew word *Zeresh* which means "Zeresh = 'gold;' the wife of Haman, the Agagite."[22]

- **Friends:** From the Hebrew word *'ahab* or *'aheb* which means "to love, human love for another, includes family, and sexual, human appetite for objects such as food, drink, sleep, wisdom, human love for or to God, act of being a friend, lover (participle), friend, God's love toward man, to individual men, to people Israel, to righteousness, lovely, loveable, friends, lovers (fig. of adulterers); to like."[23]

- **Satisfaction:** From the Hebrew word *shavah* which means "to agree with, be or become like, level, resemble."[24]

- **Recognition:** From the Hebrew word *'ahab* or *'aheb* which means "to love, human love for another, includes family, and sexual, human appetite for objects such as food, drink, sleep, wisdom, human love for or to God, act of being a friend, lover (participle), friend, God's love toward man, to individual men, to people Israel, to righteousness, lovely, loveable, friends, lovers (fig. of adulterers); to like."[25]

- **Grief:** From the Hebrew word *'abel* which means "mourning."[26]

## Esther 3:1-15

**After these events, King Xerxes honored Haman son of Hammedatha, the Agagite, elevating him and giving him a seat of honor higher than that of all the other nobles. All the royal officials at the king's gate knelt down and paid honor to Haman, for the king had commanded this concerning him. But Mordecai would not kneel down or pay him honor.**

**Then the royal officials at the king's gate asked Mordecai, "Why do you disobey the king's command?"**

Day after day they spoke to him but he refused to comply. Therefore they told Haman about it to see whether Mordecai's behavior would be tolerated, for he had told them that he was a Jew.

When Haman saw that Mordecai would not kneel down or pay him honor, he was enraged. Yet having learned who Mordecai's people were, he scorned the idea of killing only Mordecai. Instead Haman looked for a way to destroy all Mordecai's people, the Jews, throughout the whole kingdom of Xerxes.

In the twelfth year of King Xerxes, in the first month, the month of Nisan, they cast the pur (that is, the lot) in the presence of Haman to select a day and month. And the lot fell on the twelfth month, the month of Adar.

Then Haman said to King Xerxes, "There is a certain people dispersed and scattered among the peoples in all the provinces of your kingdom whose customs are different from those of all other people and who do not obey the king's laws; it is not in the king's best interest to tolerate them. If it pleases the king, let a decree be issued to destroy them, and I will put ten thousand talents of silver into the royal treasury for the men who carry out this business."

Then on the thirteenth day of the first month the royal secretaries were summoned. They wrote out in the script of each province and in the language of each people all Haman's orders to the king's satraps, the governors of the various provinces and the nobles of the various peoples. These were written in the name of King Xerxes himself and sealed with his own ring. Dispatches were sent by couriers to all the king's provinces with the order to destroy, kill, and annihilate all the Jews – young and old, women and little children – on a single day, the thirteenth day of the twelfth month, the month of Adar, and to plunder their goods. A copy of the text of the edict was to be issued as law in every province and made known to the people of every nationality so they would be ready for that day.

**Spurred on by the king's command, the couriers went out, and the edict was issued in the citadel of Susa. The king and Haman sat down to drink, but the city of Susa was bewildered.**

(Related Bible references: Proverbs 27:3, Joel 3:3, Matthew 5:22, Matthew 5:43-48, Acts 5:27-29, Romans 13:1-10)

Esther chapter 3 opens by introducing us to another character: that of Haman, a high-ranking official under King Xerxes' rule. We have no idea where he came from or how he rose to power, or where he came from. Even his ethnic origin, "Agagite," has no national or ethnic connection to any group clearly identified in history. As much as he seems to have appeared here in the Scriptures, so it would seem he appeared in history, as well. He was identified as being among the noble elite of the royal court, which, most likely, indicates he was part of an aristocracy, a governing class to which he was probably born. He was so notable, his seat of honor was higher than everyone else's, and everyone in the palace knelt in honor to him.

Everyone that was, except Mordecai who refused.

There are many different theories as to why Mordecai refused to bow before Haman in direct disobedience to royal command. Some theories include that Haman had the image of an idol on his garments, others believe it was that Haman himself became an idol and was expecting others to honor him as such, and others believe there was a much deeper, long standing personal rivalry between Mordecai and Haman's families. Whatever the reason, Mordecai absolutely refused to kneel or pay any sort of honor to Haman, and he made his position known, day after day after day, even after being called in and questioned by royal officials as to why he was acting in such disobedience. His behavior had caused quite a stir, not to mention question as to what would happen to Mordecai for such direct disrespect. The national pride of the empire was at stake, and refusing to honor such leaders could have had dire consequences. The reason there was question in the first place was because Mordecai was a Jew, and in understanding and respecting religious differences within the empire, it was uncertain if such would be protected, or not.

Mordecai sets the stage for something else within each of us, and that is an understanding of civil disobedience in the right to protest and refuse to do certain things simply because they may be law. It's easy to fall into the trap of national idolatry, worshiping the government and regulations of a nation simply because it is where one is. We can blindly follow national customs and adhere to what we feel is the easiest or most explicit of our national pride, forgetting that pride in any form can lead us into dangerous and difficult places. Mordecai knew that bowing down before Haman was wrong, and whatever his reason, he had to follow his spiritually formed conscience to do what he knew, beyond a shadow of a doubt, was right to do.

Mordecai is not the only Biblical figure who exemplified principles of civil disobedience. The Hebrew midwives, Rahab, Jonathan, Athaliah, Daniel, Shadrach, Meshach, Abednego, Peter and John all behaved in manners that were considered threatening or disobedient to civil authorities. They were believers who, in complicated situations, refused to extend and obey pressures to submit to evil rules and do things that were wrong or were, in some instances, in objection to their rights. Even though what Mordecai might have done appeared to be against the law, it is obvious from the question of how to handle things that Mordecai was exercising a right that was his to observe.

*So they brought them and set them before the council (Sanhedrin). And the high priest examined them by questioning,*

*Saying, We definitely commanded and strictly charged you not to teach in or about this Name; yet here you have flooded*

*Jerusalem with your doctrine and you intend to bring this Man's blood upon us.*

*Then Peter and the apostles replied, We must obey God rather than men.*
*(Acts 5:27-29, AMPC)*

*Let every person be loyally subject to the governing (civil) authorities. For there is no authority except from God [by His permission, His sanction], and those that exist do so by God's appointment.*

*Therefore he who resists and sets himself up against the authorities resists what God has appointed and arranged [in divine order]. And those who resist will bring down judgment upon themselves [receiving the penalty due them].*

*For civil authorities are not a terror to [people of] good conduct, but to [those of] bad behavior. Would you have no dread of him who is in authority? Then do what is right and you will receive his approval and commendation.*
*For he is God's servant for your good. But if you do wrong, [you should dread him and] be afraid, for he does not bear and wear the sword for nothing. He is God's servant to execute His wrath (punishment, vengeance) on the wrongdoer.*

*Therefore one must be subject, not only to avoid God's wrath and escape punishment, but also as a matter of principle and for the sake of conscience.*

*For this same reason you pay taxes, for [the civil authorities] are official servants under God, devoting themselves to attending to this very service.*

*Render to all men their dues. [Pay] taxes to whom taxes are due, revenue to whom revenue is due, respect to whom respect is due, and honor to whom honor is due.*

*Keep out of debt and owe no man anything, except to love one another; for he who loves his neighbor [who practices loving others] has fulfilled the Law [relating to one's fellowmen, meeting all its requirements].*

*The commandments, You shall not commit adultery, You shall not kill, You shall not steal, You shall not covet (have an evil desire), and any other commandment, are summed up in the single command, You shall love your neighbor as [you do] yourself.*

*Love does no wrong to one's neighbor [it never hurts anybody]. Therefore love meets all the requirements and is the fulfilling of the Law.*
(Romans 13:1-10, AMPC)

Today we debate over just what is permissible – and what is not – when it comes to breaking the law or disobeying civil regulation, usually citing the passage above as a reason to require citizens of a nation to submit to any rule and ruling, no matter how unjust it might have been. In so doing, I believe we are missing the Apostle Paul's point in the passage. The Apostle Paul was advising us against deliberately stirring up trouble where such wasn't necessary, thus giving the faith and the Body of believers a bad name and reputation. There is no reason to deliberately and willfully set out to disobey governmental orders, and we can all agree nobody in the examples of Biblical civil disobedience ever did such. They were ordinary individuals, minding their own business and exercising their faith as private citizens. All lived under certain laws and statutes that, for whatever reason, came into conflict with their beliefs. The conflict did not come from them, however, but from the government itself, that demanded they do something that was against their principles. When faced with a choice between exercising one's genuine conscience formed by faith and submitting to something that contradicts such, believers have the right – and the duty – to resist.

Yet Mordecai – one man, doing one thing, having one perspective and opinion about Haman – drove Haman to distraction. It's amazing that the way in which we carry ourselves as believers can bother others, even when everyone else is doing whatever it is they desire. The entire guards of the court came and knelt to honor Haman, and this one, tiny little man's refusal upset Haman so much, he put out a vendetta in response. Not only did he want Mordecai killed, he wanted all Mordecai's people – the entire Jewish population in the Persian Empire – killed.

This might sound amazing to us, but we have, most likely, been both Haman and Mordecai at different points in our lives. We've all wanted our accomplishments to be noticed and idolized by others, feeling the sting when someone took issue with whatever we were doing or seeking as a result. Something in us wanted their acknowledgement, specifically from them, and when we didn't get it, we felt scorned and upset. It didn't matter how many other people might have praised us or lauded us for what we did, all we remembered was that one person who didn't acknowledge us in the way we'd hoped. In our instance, we might harbor a resentment against that person, act out in different ways, behave unseemly, or wallow in hurt feelings and offense, but Haman had something most don't have when this arises: he had power. He had the authority to stand up and annihilate an entire group of people, for no other reason than one of them scorned him.

Haman reminds us why stereotypes and bigotries are so bad. No one person is representative of an entire populace or body of people, no matter how bad your experience might have been with them. We cannot say that everyone is a certain way or that everyone is like this or that, because that reduces life and outlook to judgment. Such attitudes have led to dangerous attempted annihilations of people throughout history, including the Holocaust, Holodomor, and genocides in Armenia, Serbia, Guatemala, Assyria, Greece, Darfur, Bosnia, and Cambodia, among others. One person angry and scorned by an individual or even a few individuals can turn into a mighty fuel and force of hate, which leads other unsuspecting people right into its lure. Hate is hate is hate, and Haman started out with a scorned attitude against one that quickly turned into bigotry against an entire group of people.

*But I say to you that everyone who continues to be angry with his brother or harbors malice (enmity of heart) against him shall be liable to and unable to escape the punishment imposed by the court; and whoever speaks contemptuously and insultingly to his brother shall be liable to and unable to escape the punishment imposed by the Sanhedrin, and whoever says, You cursed fool! [You empty-headed idiot!] shall be liable to and unable to escape the hell (Gehenna) of fire... You have heard that it was said, You shall love your neighbor and hate your enemy;*

*But I tell you, Love your enemies and pray for those who persecute you,*

*To show that you are the children of your Father Who is in heaven; for He makes His sun rise on the wicked and on the good, and makes the rain fall upon the upright and the wrongdoers [alike].*

*For if you love those who love you, what reward can you have? Do not even the tax collectors do that?*

*And if you greet only your brethren, what more than others are you doing? Do not even the Gentiles (the heathen) do that?*

*You, therefore, must be perfect [growing into complete maturity of godliness in mind and character, having reached the proper height of virtue and integrity], as your heavenly Father is perfect.*
(Matthew 5:22, 43-48 AMPC)

We've also probably been in situations that were much like that which Mordecai experienced. There will forever be things in this world that go against the grain of our faith-inspired integrity, causing us to know we must make a stand against what we are seeing, hearing, and encountering. We just do not have it within us to bow down and worship the image that has been set before us, and we refuse. The courage and integrity it takes to stand against such idolatrous culture, especially when others are doing it and we fear the threat of having to deal with harm, discomfort, or the general unpleasantness of having to answer to others for our choices. Yet in such situations, we must persevere, never compromising the dignity of our faith for something that will lead us into idolatry. This is different from compromising when we are wrong, finding solutions to problems, or just being hardheaded and difficult in the face of a changing culture or situation, and it is also different from just refusing to do something because we don't want to do it. Mordecai was moved by a conviction, by a reality of truth, and even though it wasn't what Haman sought, it was what he had to do.

Both instances call us to grow as people, no matter what end of the line we might find ourselves on. We cannot expect the entire world will celebrate everything we do, whether right or wrong, unconditionally, nor can we expect that we will be able to give in and do whatever is asked of us in every situation. They are God's way of revealing things about us and through us to all involved, and, most importantly, revealing Himself to us. What we do under pressure and how we respond when we are hurt or wounded tells much about who we are in our faith, and who God is calling us to be. Both Haman and Mordecai could have made different choices, and the choices they made reveals the difference between an ungodly character and a godly one.

The dichotomy between Haman and Mordecai continues as Haman moves forward with his plan to annihilate all Jews in the Persian Empire. They cast lots, known as "pur," to determine on what day they would move forward with their evil agenda. The lot fell on the day of 12 Adar, and such was set for a specific time to annihilate the Jews, under the guise of doing so because their customs were different and they were not following the "laws" of the land. Those who carried out the edict were to receive heavy financial compensation, not considering they were not acting at the king's command, but on behalf of the vengeance of someone who simply didn't get his way.

Haman's usurping of royal authority - commanding such a thing in the king's name, without his consult and without any consideration to anyone else - shows us that we must be very careful what we choose to involve ourselves with, whatever cause or showing we are quick to jump in and support. Haman gave just the right incentive - a large sum of money - to make sure that no one asked any questions about why he was doing what he was doing, and to make sure they would just jump in and participate. How many of us do just the same thing, thinking the incentive (be it loyalty or money) is right there? Every day on social media, in church settings, even sometimes in the workplace, we hear half of a story and are quick to cheer on whoever told that part of something without ever considering that maybe we aren't hearing the entire story. Unknowingly, we too often encourage people to house vendettas, behave unseemly, hold grudges or embitter unforgiveness, or involve people in a battle that has nothing to do with them and is in no way their business. Haman used an entire empire to go after an entire group of people because he was angry at one man. Call upon the spirit of discernment to make sure you aren't being used for such a purpose by someone because they haven't learned how to handle their own emotions or deal with someone directly, without involving everyone else. Power in the wrong hands is a dangerous thing, no matter who it is, specifically, who may have it.

As the edict went forth, the provinces were informed, the information went out, and people started to work their plan, thinking King Xerxes had made the official declaration himself. The text indicates the city of Susa was in an uproar as Haman sat back, pleased with his perceived accomplishments. I am sure other parts of the provinces were also surprised and shocked at such a direct declaration, even though we do not have a record of it. We do not have, however, any indication that anyone sought to do much about it anywhere outside of Susa. People might have been shocked and horrified, but under the guise of doing something "legal," they did nothing. Never allow a misguided sense of patriotism, legality, or national loyalty to lead you into thinking a wrong thing is a right thing. God is still God, and we still must answer to him for what we do, which makes our integrity so vital in such circumstances.

All is not lost, however, as we shall see in the following chapters. God strategically set up His people in specific places to make sure the will of God would go forth, even in the darkest of days. Always remember that God is there for you, with His strategic purpose, to assist and help you, no matter what you are going through. Instead of looking to the darkness, hear His voice, find and attend to the Mordecais and Esthers in your life, and set up strategy to overcome…even this.

## Esther 4:1-17

**When Mordecai learned of all that had been done, he tore his clothes, put on sackcloth and ashes, and went out into the city, wailing loudly and bitterly. But he went only as far as the king's gate, because no one clothed in sackcloth was allowed to enter it. In every province to which the edict and order of the king came, there was great mourning among the Jews, with fasting, weeping, and wailing. Many lay in sackcloth and ashes.**

**When Esther's maids and eunuchs came and told her about Mordecai, she was in great distress. She sent clothes for him to put on instead of his sackcloth, but he would not accept them. Then Esther summoned Hathach, one of the king's eunuchs assigned to attend her, and**

ordered him to find out what was troubling Mordecai and why.

So Hathach went out to Mordecai in the open square of the city in front of the king's gate. Mordecai told him everything that had happened to him, including the exact amount of money Haman had promised to pay into the royal treasury for the destruction of the Jews. He also gave him a copy of the text of the edict for their annihilation, which had been published in Susa, to show to Esther and explain it to her, and he told him to urge her to go into the king's presence to beg for mercy and plead with him for her people.

Hathach went back and reported to Esther what Mordecai had said. Then she instructed him to say to Mordecai, "All the king's officials and the people of the royal provinces know that for any man or woman who approaches the king in the inner court without being summoned the king has but one law: that he be put to death. The only exception to this is for the king to extend the gold scepter to him and spare his life. But thirty days have passed since I was called to go to the king."

When Esther's words were reported to Mordecai, he sent back this answer: "Do not think that because you are in the king's house you alone of all the Jews will escape. For if you remain silent at this time, relief and deliverance for the Jews will arise from another place, but you and your father's family will perish. And who knows but that you have come to royal position for such a time as this?"

Then Esther sent this reply to Mordecai: "Go, gather together all the Jews who are in Susa, and fast for me. Do not eat or drink for three days, night or day. I and my maids will fast as you do. When this is done, I will go to the king, even though it is against the law. And if I perish, I perish."

So Mordecai went away and carried out all of Esther's instructions.

(Related Bible references: Proverbs 16:15, Ezekiel 21:6, Isaiah 58:5,

Jeremiah 6:26, Ezekiel 27:30, Micah 1:8, Daniel 9:3, John 12:25, John 15:12-13)

With the edict now a part of the life of the Persian Empire, Mordecai received news of its advance and was filled with grief. It filled him with such a sense of mourning, he put on sackcloth and ashes and went through the city as if the event had already occurred, weeping and wailing in grief. Other Jews also started mourning, crying, fasting, weeping, wailing, and laying in sackcloth and ashes. No one, not even Mordecai, was allowed to go beyond the king's gate, however, because they were in sackcloth. This means even though all the Jews of Susa were engaged in heavy mourning, Xerxes still didn't know about it. Esther did not know of these matters, either, until someone came and told her about Mordecai. This should give a good idea of what life was like for those who lived in the palace, particularly the women: they were so far removed from the ordinary and everyday life of the citizens of a nation or province, they had no idea the impact of royal decisions or decrees on their subjects.

This was one of those edicts that caused a huge uproar, and when Esther found out about Mordecai, she was notably upset. She tried sending him clothes, but he refused to wear them. Then Esther summoned the assistance of another eunuch, Hathach, to find out just what was troubling Mordecai. Hathach found out all the gritty details of Haman's edict, right down to the amount of money those who would complete the job would be paid and was sent back with a copy of the edict. Esther is initially shocked, but uncertain of what to do. She knew Mordecai expected her to do something, but how to do it was of great question. If she was to go into the king without being called, she could have easily been put to death. It had been about a month since she had been called to see the king, and in the meantime, she remained in the royal palace, minding her own business. The only way she could be spared is if the king extended his gold scepter to her, sparing his life.

It is obvious that Esther didn't feel she knew Xerxes or his intentions toward her and given she probably hadn't been called in to see him very often since becoming Queen, she couldn't predict his behavior. His past behavior was highly erratic and unpredictable, and it would be unreasonable to say that Xerxes had changed in his entirety over the years. He was probably older and somewhat wiser, with more experiences and failures under his belt, but that doesn't mean he didn't have a temper and never made a rash decision. Esther's concern was for her actual ability to make an impact without losing her life, and the question of such was very, very real in the face of a ruler like Xerxes.

Esther and Xerxes weren't a romance novel. Xerxes wasn't a leading man who swept her off her feet, and Esther was not a pathetic damsel in distress. Xerxes was a warrior, a powerful military leader, who was successful in leading the large Persian Empire not because he was gentle, but because he knew how to maintain control and a sense of power. It would be ridiculous to suggest such didn't extend to his personal life (at least to some extent), and this fact was not lost on Esther. She wasn't sure what to do, and it was Mordecai who shook her back into reality. If she didn't step in, she wouldn't survive, either. Someone would find out about her history and she could die, either way, whether she said something, or did nothing. She was here for such a time as this, a phrase we invoke all the time (but don't give the first thought to the intensity of its meaning). In being there for such a time as this, God knew that Esther had what it took to do what needed to be done, and everyone and everything around her was a divine setup to make sure that God's people were spared.

So, Esther asks Mordecai and all the Jews of Susa to fast for her for three days, and she would do the same along with her maids. Mordecai, the unnamed Jews, her maids, the eunuchs, and everyone else who was involved in this process was just as important – just as much here for such a time as this – as Esther was. Those who help, those who assist, those who come along and are there to lift up, help, encourage, pray, fast, and offer support are just as relevant as those who must stand up and do the dirty work to get the job done. This massive team effort shows us just how spiritual things get done, and in more modern times, how the Gospel is preached - with those who support, those who receive, those who go, and those who help - as we all fulfil our own assignments to get the job done.

Esther's final declaration in the chapter is to go to the King, and face reality: if she perishes, she perishes. She shows intense resolve and character, but also proves she was willing to make the ultimate sacrifice for her people. This cements her position as a type of Christ, because Christ, too, was willing to make His sacrifice for the salvation of mankind. By adopting this role, and this type that she most likely did not even understand herself, Esther took on a position as a type of savior, standing in for the salvation of her people, who did not have any other hope without her intervention. This was no small thing, as she ran the risk of death for doing what was right. Esther showed her love for others, as we recognize and is seen in the work of the New Testament.

*This is my commandment, That ye love one another, as I have loved you. Greater love hath no man than this, that a man lay down his life for his friends.*
(John 15:12-13, KJV)

We read John 15:12-13 and think it's a nice principle to live by, but it seems like an impossible challenge when we start taking it out of context. Esther's courage and willingness to do what needed to be done gives us a greater perspective on just how we live our love for others. It is not so much flying in front of a whizzing bullet or forcibly killing ourselves in place of another, as it is recognizing we are here for such a time as this. If we are to live now, we recognize God has placed us as part of His plan, equipping us to function now, in this time, as much as for our neighbor as for ourselves. Christ made this sacrifice for us, Esther was willing to make that sacrifice, and as people today, we should be willing to live, to make a difference for others in this world, today. We can see from their work that evangelizing and reaching out to help others in love is about more than just talking about Jesus; it is about action, about willingness, and about sacrifice, to make sure that the work we say we uphold gets done. Esther kept her word and Mordecai followed her instructions – and as one helped the other – the love of one another was laid down for a powerful change and promise to intervene on behalf of the Jewish people.

In keeping with the principle of salvation, it is essential for us to embrace the idea of a different kind of love present in Esther. It is a sacrificial love, one that is not romantic in nature or carrying one off into any number of fairy-tale decisions, but one that does the right thing simply because it's right. Christ loved us so much He sacrificed Himself for us; and that is the true definition of love. The goal was salvation, but the point of it all was love. Esther, too, did what she did out of a sense of love, not refraining and holding herself back out of selfish gain or conceit, but doing what she did because Esther genuinely cared about her people. Being so willing to make such a sacrifice proves Esther's love for others and proves her work as a type of Christ.

## Esther 5:1-14

**On the third day Esther put on her royal robes and stood in the inner court of the palace, in front of the king's hall. The king was sitting on his royal throne in the hall, facing the entrance. When he saw Queen Esther standing in the court, he was pleased with her and held out to her the gold scepter that was in his hand. So Esther approached and touched the tip of the scepter.**

**Then the king asked, "What is it, Queen Esther? What is your request? Even up to half the kingdom, it will be given you."**

**"If it pleases the king," replied Esther, "let the king, together with Haman, come today to a banquet I have prepared for him."**

> *"Bring Haman at once," the king said, "so that we may do what Esther asks."*
>
> *So the king and Haman went to the banquet Esther had prepared. As they were drinking wine, the king again asked Esther, "Now what is your petition? It will be given you. And what is your request? Even up to half the kingdom, it will be granted."*
>
> *Esther replied, "My petition and my request is this: If the king regards me with favor and if it pleases the king to grant my petition and fulfill my request, let the king and Haman come tomorrow to the banquet I will prepare for them. Then I will answer the king's question."*
>
> *Haman went out that day happy and in high spirits. But when he saw Mordecai at the king's gate and observed that he neither rose nor showed fear in his presence, he was filled with rage against Mordecai. Nevertheless, Haman restrained himself and went home.*
>
> *Calling together his friends and Zeresh, his wife, Haman boasted to them about his vast wealth, his many sons, and all the ways the king had honored him and how he had elevated him above the other nobles and officials. "And that's not all," Haman added. "I'm the only person Queen Esther invited to accompany the king to the banquet she gave. And she has invited me along with the king tomorrow. But all this gives me no satisfaction as long as I see that Jew Mordecai sitting at the king's gate."*
>
> *His wife Zeresh and all his friends said to him, "Have a gallows build, seventy-five feet high, and ask the king in the morning to have Mordecai hanged on it. Then go with the king to the dinner and be happy." This suggestion delighted Haman, and he had the gallows built.*

(Related Bible references: Matthew 6:16-18, Mark 6:23)

Much like when she first went to meet with the king in chapter 2, Esther returns to the same practice, only a little shorter, here in chapter 5. She put on her royal robes signifying her position within the kingdom, and helping her to be identified, even from a distance. Maybe the main point is that Esther prepared herself, not just through fasting, but in practical ways, as well. She didn't just go into this monumental task in anything she had laying around. She prepared herself spiritually, she got ready physically, and she went in to do what needed to be done, preparing to risk her life if that's what it took. Taking those brave steps in, Esther poised herself for what she needed to do and went in unto the king.

*When you fast [giving up eating for spiritual purposes], don't put on a sad [gloomy; somber] face like the hypocrites. They make their faces look sad [disheveled; disfigured; unattractive] to show people they are fasting. I tell you the truth, those hypocrites already have their full reward [v. 2]. So when you fast [v. 16], comb your hair [put oil on/anoint your head; typical first century grooming] and wash your face. Then people will not know that you are fasting, but your Father, whom you cannot see [who is hidden/in secret], will see you. Your Father sees what is done in secret [private], and He will reward you.*
(Matthew 6:16-18, EXB)

A continual theme in the book of Esther is the connection between practical and the spiritual, not treating the two as if they are unrelated, but revealing their interconnected nature. Sometimes we read the words of Scripture and think that spirituality will clean everything up, won't put us in difficult or complicated places, or won't require anything practical of us. This is not the case, and just as when we are fasting, we are told to take care of our physical bodies and get our acts together, not letting everyone on to what is going on with us all the time. Esther might have been afraid, but she kept it together. She didn't let her personal state keep her from making sure everything was positioned for the best success. We, too, should aim for this goal in our own lives – to avoid becoming so spiritual that we forget we must implement our spirituality throughout our life actions.

Esther's advance into the court was a rarity for these times. Women were kept to a certain sphere, or dwelling, within palace quarters, and if the king did not call for her, she did not leave those areas specifically set apart for women. She would have had no knowledge of edict, decree, or politics, because those happened outside the quarters reserved for women. As she enters the court and Xerxes is pleased to see her, such must have come as a huge relief. She is extended the gold scepter, which means she is out of danger. The king was happy to offer Esther whatever it was she sought, anticipating her need. This unexpected shift reflects God's incredible favor upon Esther, now not just in a personal sense, but for the accomplishment of this most relevant end goal. Esther's personal character gained her favor and note among those around her, and now it was helping her to influence policy and procedure within the entire empire. The goal of favor is not just to generate something personal, but to generate something larger and more powerful in the long run.

Esther's response seems unlikely yet reveals a strategy: she desires Xerxes to attend a banquet, along with Haman, that she has prepared specifically for him. They call for Haman immediately, and Haman and Xerxes attend her banquet. During the meal, Xerxes inquires again, wanting to know what it is that she desires of him. She's assured whatever she wants, he will grant to her, but Esther still seeks to do things slowly and within order. She invites both he and Haman back for another banquet the next day, and then she would let him know what she wants from him.

Haman leaves, suspecting nothing, happy, full, and expecting he will continue to receive honors within the royal court. It only took one little glance of Mordecai to set him afire with rage, all over again, because Mordecai still refused to kneel before Haman. Ready to act, Haman instead decides to return home and discuss matters with his wife, Zeresh, and his friends. Continuing the theme of female influence in the book of Esther, it is clear that Zeresh is not just acting as a passive figure but is an active agent and advisor to Haman. She was among the first around him to bolster his ego and encourage him in his devious plots, no matter how wrong or unrighteous they may have been. Along with his friends, Zeresh is mentioned first - before all of them - indicating that her opinions and direction were of first priority, thus she had a voice and counsel that outweighed the rest. It was at her direction the lot of them recommended Mordecai be killed, via the gallows for hanging, to put an end to his constant reminder that not everyone was as enamored with Haman as he was, himself. They instructed him to go to the banquet, to be in good spirits, and to give no aforethought to it any further.

There's a lot of talk these days about having people in your corner to support you and lift you up, but there isn't a lot of talk about what support means. We indicate we should never be among people who express any criticism (because such can never be constructive) and that we should immediately cut off people who are somehow different from us or question us in some manner. Haman had a group of people around him who did exactly what everyone today seems to want - and the results were less than ideal. Haman had a "circle" that went with whatever he wanted and supported a view of himself that was both ungodly and not helpful to him in the long run. Instead of telling him the truth and supporting his change, they encouraged his self-worship and idolatry.

There's a difference between not having someone's back and being so blind to someone's behavior that you let them fall into a pit. Zeresh and Haman's friends probably felt untouchable, and believed if Haman could ascend the heights, so could they. While I don't advise we go around demeaning our friends and close family, we can realize there is a difference between being a bully and caring enough about someone to let them know their path, their attitude, or their current collision course will end in disaster. Haman's friends didn't love, nor care about him enough to help him be better. As we see what happens to Haman, let us never be the kind of friends who let others fall because it is simply easier to hope their advancement will provide something for our personal gain.

## **Esther 6:1-14**

*That night the king could not sleep; so he ordered the book of the chronicles, the record of his reign, to be brought in and read to him. It was found recorded there that Mordecai had exposed Bigthana and Teresh, two of the king's officers who guarded the doorway, who had conspired to assassinate King Xerxes.*

*"What honor and recognition has Mordecai received for this?" the king asked.*

*"Nothing has been done for him," his attendants answered.*

*The king said, "Who is in the court?" Now Haman had just entered the outer court of the palace to speak to the king about hanging Mordecai on the gallows he had erected for him.*

*His attendants answered, "Haman is standing in the court."*

*"Bring him in," the king ordered.*

*When Haman entered, the king asked him, "What should be done for the man the king delights to honor?"*

*Now Haman thought to himself, "Who is there that the king would rather honor than me?" So he answered the king, "For the man the king delights to honor, have them bring a royal robe the king has worn and a horse the king has ridden, one with a royal crest placed on its head. Then let the robe and horse be entrusted to one of the king's most noble princes. Let them robe the man the king delights to honor, and lead him on the horse through the city streets, proclaiming before him. 'This is what is done for the man the king delights to honor!'"*

*"Go at once," the king commanded Haman. "Get the robe and the horse and do just as you have suggested for Mordecai the Jew, who sits at the king's gate. Do not neglect anything you have recommended."*

> *So Haman got the robe and the horse. He robed Mordecai, and led him on horseback through the city streets, proclaiming before him, "This is what is done for the man the king delights to honor!"*
>
> *Afterward Mordecai returned to the king's gate. But Haman rushed home, with his head covered in grief, and told Zeresh his wife and all his friends everything that had happened to him.*
>
> *His advisers and his wife Zeresh said to him, "Since Mordecai, before whom your downfall has started, is of Jewish origin, you cannot stand against him – you will surely come to ruin!" While they were still talking with him, the king's eunuchs arrived and hurried Haman away to the banquet Esther had prepared.*

(Related Bible references: Proverbs 3:35, Proverbs 15:33, Proverbs 16:18, Proverbs 18:2, Proverbs 21:21, Hosea 14:9, Luke 14:11)

We continue in Esther chapter 6 to see the unveiling of God's plot and the unraveling of Haman's evil work. Now Xerxes, who has not shown much of a spiritual side or a direction, is disquieted one night and goes to review the record of his leadership. Such books, called records or chronicles, detailed the workings, laws, edicts, and actions of a governmental leader in any given time frame. When Xerxes saw firsthand the work of Mordecai in preventing the plot to assassinate him, he was moved with a sense of realization that could have only come from God Himself. We can hope – and believe – that Esther's notable character opened a door for a movement of divine inspiration, even though Xerxes was not a believer. Mordecai ensured Bigthana and Teresh were not successful, and even though he did something so vital and revolutionary, he never received any accolade or credit for preventing the assassination. While asking the men of the court about this, Haman comes in, at just the perfect time, to ask what the best course of action should be to honor a great man in the kingdom. Haman naturally assumes it must be for him, so he pulls out no stops in his advice: The man should receive a royal robe and horse and rode throughout the city in a parade, letting all know that this is what happens to a man who is honorable and respectable before Xerxes. Haman is told to immediately go and find Mordecai and pay this great and royal honor to him.

*The wise will inherit honor, but fools get disgrace.*
(Proverbs 3:35, ESV)

*The fear of the Lord is instruction in wisdom, and humility comes before honor.*
(Proverbs 15:33, ESV)

*Whoever pursues righteousness and kindness will find life, righteousness, and honor.*
(Proverbs 21:21, ESV)

This is the point in the movie where the "whomp, whomp" music sounds. Haman, expecting all to be done for him, has to now go and bestow the honors he believed were for himself for a man he despised as an enemy. Getting through it was agonizing, and Haman covered himself up in grief to return home to Zeresh, his wife, and his friends for advice. Amazingly enough, this circle of people who were all too happy to promote and encourage Haman's negative behavior now don't know what to do or say. The only thing they could say - your downfall has started, and you can't take on or try to kill Mordecai, as you would, then, completely come to ruin.

Haman doesn't have much time to think about what is coming next, as the king's eunuchs come forth to sweep him away to Esther's banquet. One can only imagine he must have felt deeply lost, betrayed by his own friends and wife who are no longer providing good insight or support for his nature and character, and are encouraging him to back off without any suggestion of what should follow. Things moved fast for Haman, and a rise that most likely took a lifetime anticipates a quick fall.

No matter where we start out in life, no matter how high we rise, no matter how invincible we might feel or think ourselves, every one of us can wind up like Haman if we turn ourselves into idols and live by a vehement sense of pride and arrogance that no man can tame. It doesn't matter if we are a millionaire tycoon or a minister with an attitude - we can all fall and find ourselves where our circles of support no longer have words to uphold us any longer. We live in a world of Hamans…and in response to such, we should stand as Mordecais and Esthers, strategizing to do what is right and awaiting that time when our enemies are carried out, and we are carried in - this time, by a divine royal decree - one that is truly out of this world and all it offers.

# CHAPTER EIGHT
Celebrating Female Bravery (and All Who Helped)
(Esther Chapters 7-10)

## **Key verses**

- **Chapter 7 verses 3-6:** *Then Queen Esther answered, "If I have found favor with you, O king, and if it pleases your majesty, grant me my life - this is my petition. And spare my people - this is my request. For I and my people have been sold for destruction and slaughter and annihilation. If we had merely been sold as male and female slaves, I would have kept quiet, because no such distress would justify disturbing the king." King Xerxes asked Queen Esther, "Who is he? Where is the man who has dared to do such a thing?" Esther said, "The adversary and enemy is this vile Haman." Then Haman was terrified before the king and queen.*

- **Chapter 8 verses 7-8:** *King Xerxes replied to Queen Esther and to Mordecai the Jew, "Because Haman attacked the Jews, I have given his estate to Esther, and they have hanged him on the gallows. Now write another decree in the king's name in behalf of the Jews as seems best to you, and seal it with the king's signet ring - for no document written in the king's name and sealed with his ring can be revoked."*

- **Chapter 8 verses 11-12:** *The king's edict granted the Jews in every city the right to assemble and protect themselves; to destroy, kill, and annihilate any armed force of any nationality or province that might attack them and their women and children; and to plunder the property of their enemies. The day appointed for the Jews to do this in all the provinces of King Xerxes was the thirteenth day of the twelfth month, the month of Adar.*

- **Chapter 8 verses 15-17:** *Mordecai left the king's presence wearing royal garments of blue and white, a large crown of gold and a purple robe of fine linen. And the city of Susa held a joyous celebration. For the Jews it was a time of happiness and joy, gladness and honor. In every province and in every city, wherever the edict of the king went, there was joy and gladness among the Jews, with feasting and celebrating. And many people of other nationalities became Jews because fear of the Jews had seized them.*

- **Chapter 9 verses 20-26:** *Mordecai recorded these events, and he sent letters to all the Jews throughout the provinces of King Xerxes, near and far, to have them celebrate annually the fourteenth and fifteenth days of the month of Adar as the time when the Jews got relief from their enemies, and as the month when their sorrow was turned into joy and their mourning into a day of celebration. He wrote them to observe the days as days of feasting and joy and giving presents of food to one another and gifts to the poor. So the Jews agreed to continue the celebration they had begun, doing what Mordecai had written to them. For Haman son of Hammedatha, the Agagite, the enemy of all the Jews, had plotted against the Jews to destroy them and had cast the pur (that is, the lot) for their ruin and destruction. But when the plot came to* *the king's attention, he issued written orders that the evil scheme Haman had devised against the Jews should come back on his own head, and that he and his sons should be hanged on the gallows. Therefore these days were called Purim, from the word pur.)*

## Words and phrases to know

- **Request:** From the Hebrew word *she'elah* or *shelah* (1 Sam 1:17) which means "request, thing asked for, demand."[1]

- **Adversary and enemy:** From two Hebrew words: *tsar* or *tsar* which means "narrow, tight; straits, distress; adversary, foe, enemy, oppressor; hard pebble, flint"[2] and *'oyeb* or *'owyeb* which means "enemy."[3]

- **Molest:** From the Hebrew word *kabash* which means "to subject, subdue, force, keep under, bring into bondage."[4]

- **Harbona:** From the Hebrew word *Charbowna'* or *Charbownah* which means "Harbona or Harbonah = 'ass-driver;' the 3rd of the seven chamberlains or eunuchs who served Ahasuerus."[5]

- **Joyous:** From the Hebrew word *sameach* which means "joyful, merry, glad."[6]

- **Parshandatha:** From the Hebrew word *Parshandatha'* which means "Parshandatha = 'given by prayer;' one of the 10 sons of Haman the enemy of Mordecai and queen Esther."[7]

- **Dalphon:** From the Hebrew word *Dalphown* which means "Dalphon = 'dripping;' the second of the 10 sons of Haman."[8]

- **Aspatha:** From the Hebrew word *'Acpatha'* which means "Aspatha = 'the enticed gathered;' the third son of Haman."[9]

- **Poratha:** From the Hebrew word *Powratha'* which means "Poratha = 'fruitfulness' or 'frustration;' one of the ten sons of Haman, the enemy of Mordecai and Esther."[10]

- **Adalia:** From the Hebrew word *'Adalya'* which means "Adalia = 'I shall be drawn up of Jah;' fifth son of Haman, executed at same time."[11]

- **Aridatha:** From the Hebrew word *'Ariydatha'* which means "Aridatha = 'the lion of the decree;' a son of Haman."[12]

- **Parmashta:** From the Hebrew word *Parmashta'* which means "Parmashta = 'superior;' one of the 10 sons of Haman, the enemy of Mordecai and queen Esther."[13]

- **Arisai:** From the Hebrew word *'Ariycay* which means "Arisai = 'lion of my banners;' a son of Haman."[14]

- **Aridai:** From the Hebrew word *'Ariyday* which means "Aridai = 'the lion is enough;' a son of Haman."[15]

- **Vaizatha:** From the Hebrew word *Vayezatha'* which means "Vajezatha = 'strong as the wind;' one of the 10 sons of Haman who were hanged with their father."[16]

- **Purim:** From the Hebrew word *Puwr* also *Puwriym* or *Puriym* which means "Pur or Purim = 'lot' or 'piece;' lot, a special feast among the post-exilic Jews, to celebrate their deliverance from Haman's destruction through queen Esther's heroic actions."[17]

- **Authority:** From the Hebrew word *toqeph* which means "authority, power, strength, energy."[18]

- **Goodwill:** From the Hebrew word *shalowm* or *shalom* which means "completeness, soundness, welfare, peace."[19]

- **Assurance:** From the Hebrew word *'emeth* which means "firmness, faithfulness, truth; in truth, truly."[20]

## Esther 7:1-10

*So the king and Haman went to dine with Queen Esther, and as they were drinking wine on that second day, the king again asked, "Queen Esther, what is your petition? It will be given you. What is your request? Even up to half the kingdom, it will be granted."*

*Then Queen Esther answered, "If I have found favor with you, O king, and if it pleases your majesty, grant me my life - this is my petition. And spare my people - this is my request. For I and my people have been sold for destruction and slaughter and annihilation. If we had merely been sold as male and female slaves, I would have kept quiet, because no such distress would justify disturbing the king."*

*King Xerxes asked Queen Esther, "Who is he? Where is the man who has dared to do such a thing?"*

*Esther said, "The adversary and enemy is this vile Haman."*

*Then Haman was terrified before the king and queen. The king got up in a rage, left his wine and went out into the palace garden. But Haman, realizing that the king had already decided his fate, stayed behind to beg Queen Esther for his life.*

*Just as the king returned from the palace garden to the banquet hall, Haman was falling on the couch where Esther was reclining.*

*The king exclaimed, "Will he even molest the queen*

*while she is with me in the house?"*

*As soon as the word left the king's mouth, they covered Haman's face. Then Harbona, one of the eunuchs attending the king, said, "A gallows seventy-five feet high stands by Haman's house. He had made it for Mordecai, who spoke up to help the king."*

*The king said, "Hang him on it!" So they hanged Haman on the gallows he had prepared for Mordecai. Then the king's fury subsided.*

(Related Bible references: Psalm 9:15, Psalm 27:2, Psalm 59:12-13, Psalm 69:22, Psalm 112:10, Proverbs 14:19, 1 Corinthians 4:20, James 2:14-17)

The plot thickens as the wise Esther strategically takes down the wicked and file Haman, a man who was out for his own intentions and gains. Now at their second banquet, Esther speaks up, having awaited the proper time. Haman had had some wine, was enjoying some food, they were enjoying the evening and now was a great time to speak up and state exactly what was needed. Having had some experience now with Xerxes, Esther knew what to do and when to get the most favorable results. Instead of just blurting out anything she thought or felt, she maintained her strategy, never giving it away, and maintaining a certain sense of composure.

Waiting is sometimes the hardest part of any spiritual process, and I am sure that in Esther's case, it was no different. As these scenarios unfolded, the people behind them had to deal with the intense pressures of thought, maintaining silence, and seeking divine direction to formulate a necessary plan. It was no easier than it is for any of us, there was no secret formula or trick to the process; it had to unfold in its own time, each strategic step revealed and executed with precision. When we go through these situations, how do we handle them? Are we quick to tell everyone our secret plan or blurt out every upcoming anticipation, or can we wait with patience, knowing things will work out as they should if we will but trust God?

Esther revealed her intention – the salvation of her

people, as well as of her, personally, who were set for slaughter, destruction, and annihilation on account of Haman's evil plan. Shocked and horrified that such a thing would be done in the kingdom, Xerxes immediately wants to know who has acted for such an evil plot in his name. Discovering it was Haman, Xerxes goes out to work on his anger, and Haman seeks to plead for his life. Now that his plan has turned on him, Haman's dramatic and overdone nature threw himself on Esther's reclining couch, only to have Xerxes mistake his actions for assault or molestation against Esther. Still angry and finding Haman's continued behavior inconceivable, Xerxes immediately calls for Haman to be taken out as a criminal, his face covered and then finds himself hanging on the gallows he had built for Mordecai.

What we do has a funny way of coming back to haunt us, and the Scriptures are clear that the traps we set for others can easily be our downfall.

*For the sin of their mouths, the words of their lips,*
  *let them be trapped in their pride.*
*For the cursing and lies that they utter,*
  *consume them in wrath;*
  *consume them till they are no more,*
*that they may know that God rules over Jacob*
  *to the ends of the earth. Selah*
(Psalm 59:12-13, ESV)

Let their own table before them become a snare; and when they are at peace, let it become a trap.
(Psalm 69:22, ESV)

We should never, ever find ourselves to be so proud, so vain, and so full of ourselves that we forget nobody is untouchable. The mighty can always fall, the rich can always become poor, the plots of the wicked can always fall. There can always be a woman – or a man – who is willing to put their ear to the spiritual door of heaven and find out just how to be the willing vessel of the Lord to take down a messy person who seeks to do nothing but bring about harm and ruin. In this instance, it was the courageous Esther, a woman who let her ordinary, everyday faith position her in a place of power to do something about the evils around her.

*For the Kingdom of God is not a matter of talk, but of power.*
(1 Corinthians 4:20)

*What good is it, my brothers, if someone says he has faith but does not have works? Can that faith save him? If a brother or sister is poorly clothed and lacking in daily food, and one of you says to them, "Go in peace, be warmed and filled," without giving them the things needed for the body, what good is that? So also faith by itself, if it does not have works, is dead.*
(James 2:14-17, ESV)

What do you believe your faith can position you do to – and how does God desire to inspire you through looking at Esther's work and character? Her life proves that faith without works is truly dead, and that if we want to be people who are alive, we must be willing to put our faith where our mouths are and start doing, being, and living as people equipped for excellence and greatness in every area of our lives.

## Esther 8:1-17

**That same day King Xerxes gave Queen Esther the estate of Haman, the enemy of the Jews. And Mordecai came into the presence of the king, for Esther had told how he was related to her. The king took off his signet ring, which he had reclaimed from Haman, and presented it to Mordecai. And Esther appointed him over Haman's estate.**
    **Esther again pleaded with the king, falling at his feet and weeping. She begged him to put an end to the evil plan of Haman the Agagite, which he had devised against**

the Jews. Then the king extended the gold scepter to Esther and she arose and stood before him.

"If it pleases the king," she said, "and if he regards me with favor and thinks it the right thing to do, and if he is pleased with me, let an order be written overruling the dispatches that Haman son of Hammedatha, the Agagite, devised and wrote to destroy the Jews in all the king's provinces. For how can I bear to see disaster fall on my people? How can I bear to see the destruction of my family?"

King Xerxes replied to Queen Esther and to Mordecai the Jew, "Because Haman attacked the Jews, I have given his estate to Esther, and they have hanged him on the gallows. Now write another decree in the king's name in behalf of the Jews as seems best to you, and seal it with the king's signet ring – for no document written in the king's name and sealed with his ring can be revoked."

At once the royal secretaries were summoned – on the twenty-third day of the third month, the month of Sivan. They wrote out all Mordecai's orders to the Jews, and to the satraps, governors and nobles of the 127 provinces stretching from India to Cush. These orders were written in the script of each province and the language of each people and also to the Jews in their own script and language. Mordecai wrote in the name of King Xerxes, sealed the dispatches with the king's signet ring, and sent them by mounted couriers, who rode fast horses especially bred for the king.

The king's edict granted the Jews in every city the right to assemble and protect themselves; to destroy, kill and annihilate any armed force of any nationality or province that might attack them and their women and children; and to plunder the property of their enemies. The day appointed for the Jews to do this in all the provinces of King Xerxes was the thirteenth day of the twelfth month, the month of Adar. A copy of the text of the edict was to be issued as law in every province and *made known to the people of every nationality so that the Jews would be ready on that day to avenge themselves on their enemies.*

*The couriers, riding the royal horses, raced out, spurred on by the king's command. And the edict was also issued in the citadel of Susa.*

*Mordecai left the king's presence wearing royal garments of blue and white, a large crown of gold and a purple robe of fine linen. And the city of Susa held a joyous celebration. For the Jews it was a time of happiness and joy, gladness and honor. In every province and in every city, wherever the edict of the king went, there was joy and gladness among the Jews, with feasting and celebrating. And many people of other nationalities became Jews because fear of the Jews had seized them.*

(Related Bible references: Exodus 15:9, Daniel 2:48, Daniel 6:8, Zechariah 8:23, Galatians 3:13, Ephesians 6:10-16, Hebrews 10:25-26, 2 Peter 3:9)

The story of Esther doesn't have a quick or rapid wrap-up. While it deals with a few different instances and incidents, they all interconnect in order to bring about a specific desired result. At the firm center of our story lies Esther, now Queen Esther, who has interceded on behalf of the Jewish people to prevent their annihilation by Haman. One of the reasons why it may seem like the story is heavy on every little detail is to show the promise of God's hand in every step, as the people involved became part of God's plan. The other reason is to show us that God's plans unfold slowly. Recognizing the book of Esther takes place over a ten-year period, with a four-year gap between the first and second chapters should cause us all to take note that God just doesn't move with the same fervor that many of us do. Sure, we love that God is slow to anger when the story is about us, but we get really impatient when we are on the other end of things. Esther reminds us to walk gracefully as a royal woman, in and out of circumstances that might frighten or anger us in the natural as we move with the divine pace of our faith as God calls us to strategically move through our situations.

*The Lord does not delay and is not tardy or slow about what He promises, according to some people's conception of slowness, but He is long-suffering (extraordinarily patient) toward you, not desiring that any should perish, but that all should turn to repentance.*
(2 Peter 3:9, AMPC)

The "other side" of God's pace is always the hope of repentance. While we might want to swoop in and change everything immediately, God gives everyone in a situation time to repent before He issues any sort of action or judgment. At any time in the story of Esther, anyone could have changed their ways. Haman could have found a new path, he could have decided to let things go with Mordecai, his wife could have tried to shock him into reality, his friends could have encouraged him to do things differently, and all the others involved in the story could have chosen to do different things. On the same note, God could have struck Haman dead if he so chose without the intervention of Esther, Mordecai, Xerxes, and the rest of the individuals who were involved in the monumental shift on behalf of the Jewish people. Doing that, however, would not have allowed for Haman's repentance, nor would it have had the same impact as it did on the way things happened.

In each situation we find ourselves in, God is speaking through them – just as much to the outcome as to the process – while we are involved and engaged in it. Paying attention, being attune to what God wants us to learn (way before we reach the end of a situation) helps to enlighten us as we go along. It shows us what God desires us to turn away from, turn toward, and continue along to as we walk with Him through the difficulties we may encounter. Just as Haman had a choice to repent, so did Esther have the choice to avoid the whole situation and run from what she knew was right to do, Mordecai could have decided to kneel before Haman, Xerxes could have rejected Esther's request - but they did not. In Esther, we see a God Who is not slow, but sincerely on time - not taking the short way around anything, but recognizing every situation with foresight, insight, and seeing the end from the beginning in the entire situation.

This reveals much to us as to why a woman is the center of the story, and why women are the heroines of the book of Esther. Through many years of life, living, discerning, watching God move in situations, and learning how to give everyone time to do whatever it is that needs doing, many women (especially throughout history) have lived and embraced God in this very manner. The book of Esther reveals this intimately feminine perspective of God: detailed, true to form, consistent, patient, and unveiling patterns of purpose and devotion, not random or haphazard, that show our Father God in the carefully interwoven details of human relationships and interactions. Yes, we all understand God's hand in the picture of creation and salvation, but we sometimes forget to see God's hand in the interpersonal side of life. Esther unveils a uniquely female characteristic - that of relationship - between people in our spiritual lives. Nothing, nothing that happens is void of spiritual purpose, and absolutely nothing has to be void of spiritual interaction. If we will only listen and recognize, we will see God at work on our behalf in so many different ways, with a powerful transformation into the insights of our lives.

Now that Haman has died, there is still work left to be done; work, one will argue, that cannot go undone. His estate has been given to Queen Esther as a recompense, and his signet ring, the ring he used to execute his evil plan to begin with, has been given to Mordecai. Haman is now out of the picture, but his edict still lives on and still requires outside intervention to quell its evil. Evil deeds and actions can live on for generations if they are not stopped, and through Esther's intervention, stopping matters is exactly what will happen. Begging and pleading with Xerxes to stop

Haman's edict, Esther requests an edict to reverse the order. More than merely reversing the order, the Jews were specifically granted certain rights that upheld their status. They passed from being a merely occupied people to being individuals with certain privileges of citizenship:

- The right to assemble in and protect themselves.

- The right to defend themselves, even unto death, when someone seeks to attack them.

- To plunder the property of their enemies.

How do we parallel these specified rights to our modern-day situation as believers? While some Christians in the world do live under occupied circumstances, to have such specific rights and regulations outlined would be uncommon, if nonexistent. Christians who live in secular or Christian nations themselves would not experience the imposition of occupation, so what do these words mean for us? First and foremost, they call us to remember the rights of those who are among us who may be of minority, occupied, or otherwise small groups who don't always get the rights and privileges of citizenship that they might deserve. Just because a group is small does not mean a larger group has the right to intimidate or bully them for gain or hate purposes. Whether different from our own beliefs or not, we should never, ever think that such behavior is appropriate for people in power, and we can clearly see from the Scriptures that when a group is somehow oppressed, they have the right to liberate themselves and defend themselves against their oppressors.

In a more specified sense, we also can see certain parallels to our current spiritual citizenship as citizens of heaven, here on earth in God's Kingdom:

- As believers, we have the right to assemble, and we are encouraged to exercise that right. We should not use the times or the situations we find ourselves in as an excuse not to assemble together (Hebrews 10:25-26). This is far more than just about "going to church" as a weekly obligation. The Scriptures illuminate the world of gathering for us: group events, consecrations, convocations, holy assemblies, fellowship and mutual support, study, worship, prayer, praise, and encouragement and edification. There are so many ways this is accomplished, and we should intensely seek opportunities to connect with other believers and develop the relevant connections and insights to help one another on this mutual spiritual journey.

- We also have the encouragement of developing our strategies related to spiritual warfare, gathering for such purposes and education, and to fight independently (Ephesians 6:10-16). We have the right to fight for our spiritual rights and our continued spiritual survival. This requires us to know how to fight effectively in spiritual battle and have a reasonable understanding of how spiritual warfare impacts us. As believers, it is our right to defeat our spiritual enemy.

- Plundering is an old term for taking a defeated enemy's property as part of the spoils of war. Such was a sign, or proof, that an enemy had been defeated. While we can't go around taking things from other people, we can receive back all that was stolen from us in a spiritual sense, according to the Scriptures (Exodus 22:1-4, Job 20:18, Provers 6:30-31). If we stay with God, we shall receive recompense for anything we have lost. It might not be the same, but it will be there well enough for us to say that God has moved on our behalf.

The couriers went out and Mordecai's stature was notable: he was dressed as a royal official in the best garments, with the royal colors, celebrating his status and position with the Jews of Susa. The Jews celebrated and others became Jews out of amazement for their status and experience, because what happened to them became a testimony to others around them. They stood firm and stood upon their edict, and this told others they were serious about who they were and the God they serve. Testimony is clearly more than just telling a story; it is living it. Esther reminds us of the power of living and interactive testimony, and that as we trust God, He gives us an experience to have.

What experience do you have with God - and how is it impacting your testimony? The story shouldn't end with your battle, just as we can see the story doesn't end here - it should end with your resurrection experience, which for the Jews of Persia, is soon to come.

## Esther 9:1-17

**On the thirteenth day of the twelfth month, the month of Adar, the edict commanded by the king was to be carried out. On this day the enemies of the Jews had hoped to overpower them, but now the tables were turned and the Jews got the upper hand over those who hated them. The Jews assembled in their cities in all the provinces of King Xerxes to attack those seeking their destruction. No one could stand against them, because the people of all the other nationalities were afraid of them. And all the nobles of the provinces, the satraps, the governors and the king's administrators helped the Jews, because fear of Mordecai had seized them. Mordecai was prominent in the palace; his reputation spread throughout the provinces, and he became more powerful.**

**The Jews struck down all their enemies with the sword, killing and destroying them, and they did what they pleased to those who hated them. In the citadel of Susa, the Jews killed and destroyed five hundred men. They also killed Parshandatha, Dalphon, Aspatha, Poratha, Adalia, Aridatha, Parmashta, Arisai, Aridai and**

*Vaizatha, the ten sons of Haman son of Hammedatha, the enemy of the Jews. But they did not lay their hands on the plunder.*

*The number of those slain in the citadel of Susa was reported to the king that same day. The king said to Queen Esther, "The Jews have killed and destroyed five hundred men and the ten sons of Haman in the citadel of Susa. What have they done in the rest of the king's provinces? Now what is your petition? It will be given you. What is your request? It will also be granted."*

*"If it pleases the king," Esther answered, "give the Jews in Susa permission to carry out this day's edict tomorrow also, and let Haman's ten sons be hanged on gallows."*

*So the king commanded that this be done. An edict was issued in Susa, and they hanged the ten sons of Haman. The Jews in Susa came together on the fourteenth day of the month of Adar, and they put to death in Susa three hundred men, but they did not lay their hands on the plunder.*

*Meanwhile, the remainder of the Jews who were in the king's provinces also assembled to protect themselves and get relief from their enemies. They killed seventy-five thousand of them but did not lay their hands on the plunder. This happened on the thirteenth day of the month of Adar, and on the fourteenth they rested and made it a day of feasting and joy.*

(Related Bible references: Deuteronomy 21:22, Deuteronomy 28:13, Psalm 58:10, Psalm 71:24, Micah 5:8, Galatians 3:13, 2 Thessalonians 1:6)

As the story of Esther starts to wind up, it is an amazing testament to the way that God can change any situation that may exist, with one very important reality to God's change: God works by changing us. So many of us sit and hope for a miracle to fall out of the sky and transform things without expecting to undergo change. If Esther had sat back and asked God to change things without her intervention, it wouldn't have worked. She would have been praying for something that never would have come, because intervening on behalf of the Jewish people was her responsibility, her assignment. She was the one God desired to use to change the situation at hand.

There used to be an old saying I would hear many of the older saints say: "Lord, whatever you're doing in this season, don't do it without me!" It's something we've heard, but whenever we say it, do we realize what we are saying - and asking of God when we quote it? We can't want to be a part of whatever it is that God is doing in this season and then take no responsibility to fill the assignments He has for us in this time. Every single one of us should ask God what we are assigned to do - and see those assignments through - to be a part of the change that God wants to do. We are all here for such a time as this, and our responsibility requires us to recognize that time and our part in it to see the positive results.

The Jews had the full right to conquer their enemies, and conquer them, they did. Mordecai's place became a powerful symbol of Jewish status in the Persian Empire, and as the Scriptures state, they were the head, and not the tail.

*And the Lord shall make thee the head, and not the tail; and thou shalt be above only, and thou shalt not be beneath; if that thou hearken unto the commandments of the Lord thy God, which I command thee this day, to observe and to do them.*
(Deuteronomy 28:13, KJV)

Being the head and not the tail came with (and still comes with) a huge level of responsibility. Being the "head and not the tail" is a position of leadership, and in the case of ancient Israel and the Hebrew people, it related to moral, as well as practical, leadership. They all, as a group, were required to stand up for something that was greater than themselves and follow that leading unto the very end, wherever it took them. Mordecai, Esther, and all the Jews ready for battle had to fulfill their duties, and the result of those duties was that others around them saw all they could be. People wanted to be them, they wanted their rights and societal entitlements, and they wanted to experience the authority…but did they desire the responsibility that came along with all that? Every Jew had difficult decisions to make, and such comes along with the privilege of having such a position among groups or nations.

We might hear "we are the head, and not the tail" in our churches today, but do we recognize the important and difficult decisions we are forced to make when we are in leadership positions? The issues we face may not be life or death, as we see in the instances of the Jews of Persia, but people will come to us with just as much fire, intensity, and drive, leaving us to make very relevant and difficult decisions. Leadership, positions of authority, and being "in charge" aren't just cute things people do to pass the time quickly. When those hard situations come up, it is the leader who must decide just what is done.

Christ's sacrifice led us all out of sin and into spiritual freedom. Esther's sacrifice led to the freedom of her people, who were now free to stand up and live and worship among the Persian Empire. By taking and risking that sacrifice, she led her people to freedom. Both won the victory over Satan, doing what they were called to do, in that hour, at that appointed time. Esther stood as a leader, as one willing to do these difficult things, and see that they would be done completely, through to the end, risking all to make sure what needed doing got done. This is why the honor of Mordecai and Esther is so important. They led a people among them through difficult decisions to see even Haman's lineage wiped out. The hate, the instructions of hate, the evil that had the potential to change the face of history dissipated in one final move. The result of their stand, of doing what needed to be done, was a day of feasting and joy, but such only came after the difficult, hard, and challenging work was done. If you want to rejoice, see the feasting and joy, then you must first get to the work. We thank God for leaders like Esther and Mordecai, who are willing to stand through the challenges to get through to the joy, to the day when the brightness rises again, and everyone can visibly see the results of the challenges God's people have faced.

## Esther 9:18-32

*The Jews in Susa, however, had assembled on the thirteenth and fourteenth, and then on the fifteenth they rested and made it a day of feasting and joy.*

*That is why rural Jews - those living in villages - observe the fourteenth of the month of Adar as a day of joy and feasting, a day for giving presents to each other.*

*Mordecai recorded these events, and he sent letters to all the Jews throughout the provinces of King Xerxes, near and far, to have them celebrate annually the fourteenth and fifteenth days of the month of Adar as the time when the Jews got relief from their enemies, and as the month when their sorrow was turned into joy and their mourning into a day of celebration. He wrote them to observe the days as days of feasting and joy and giving presents of food to one another and gifts to the poor.*

*So the Jews agreed to continue the celebration they had begun, doing what Mordecai had written to them. For Haman son of Hammedatha, the Agagite, the enemy of all the Jews, had plotted against the Jews to destroy them and cast the pur (that is, the lot) for their ruin and destruction. But when the plot came to the king's attention, he issued written orders that the evil scheme Haman had devised against the Jews should come back on his own head, and that he and his sons should be hanged on the gallows. )Therefore these days were called Purim, from the word pur). Because of everything written in this letter and because of what they had seen and what had happened to them, the Jews took it upon themselves to establish the custom that they and their descendants and all who join them should without fail observe these two days every year, in the way prescribed and at the time appointed. These days should be remembered and observed in every generation by every family, and in every province and in every city. And these days of Purim should never cease to be celebrated by the Jews, nor should the memory of them die out among their descendants.*

*So Queen Esther, daughter of Abihail, along with Mordecai the Jews, wrote with full authority to confirm this second letter concerning Purim. And Mordecai sent letters to all the Jews in the 127 Provinces of the kingdom of Xerxes – words of goodwill and assurance – to establish these days of Purim at their designated times, as Mordecai the Jew and Queen Esther had decreed for them, and as they had established for themselves and their descendants in regard to their times of fasting and lamentation. Esther's decree confirmed these regulations about Purim, and it was written down in the records.*

(Related Bible references: Nehemiah 8:10, Psalm 118:15, Psalm 124:6, Psalm 141:10, Psalm 145:7, Proverbs 11:10, Joel 2:12)

The remainder of Esther Chapter 9 details the establishment of the feast of Purim, which is probably a large part of the reason the book of Esther was included in the Biblical canon. The feast of Purim is separate from the other Old Testament feasts that were a part of the required annual feasts and observances and came about in direct relation to the experience of the Jews in the book of Esther. Because Purim is not a part of the required feasts, it is almost never studied for its spiritual value. Yet as we have already established, the work and role of Esther as a type of Christ means the entire spiritual experience in the book of Esther is not some random occurrence. The same is true of the feast of Purim, which is celebrated by Jews to this very day.

The feast of Purim is a feast of overcoming and acknowledges the entire story of Esther and those around her (especially Mordecai) in the victory of the edict of Persia.

The word "Purim" is from the Persian word, "pur," which means "lot." It is named after the lots that Haman cast to determine his day for destruction of the Jewish people. Purim is typically observed in the Spring, somewhere between the end of February and April, each year. For those who are unaware of the details of this observance, Purim contains the following elements:[21]

- Reading the book of Esther (known as the Megillah Scroll in Judaism) on the eve of Purim and then again on the following day. When Haman's name is mentioned, all are encouraged to sound noisemakers or stamp their feet to erase his name from the record.

- Giving gifts, specifically money, to at least two poor people.

- Sending at least two different kinds of food to at least one person.

- A Purim festival or feast, which includes wine and other intoxicants. This is usually done with a meal in the home, and features bread, meat, wine, Jewish songs, and sayings from the Old Testament.

- Children (and sometimes adults) wear festive costumes to teach on the miracle of Purim, because the hand of God was seen disguised as natural events.

- Before Purim, special readings are held in synagogue to recall the evil deeds of Haman's ancestors and most Jews fast on the day before Purim, just as the maids and Mordecai fasted along with Esther as she prepared to go to the king.

- In ancient walled cities, such as Jerusalem, Purim is celebrated a day after it is celebrated elsewhere, being observed on the 15th of Adar. This commemorates the tradition of Purim's observance a day later in walled cities.

The victory of Purim came because of Esther, who was willing to do the ultimate. In her work, life overcame death. Purim, therefore, stands as our eternal battle between life and death: a type of the resurrection, as well as a greater type of eternity after Jesus Christ returns. On Purim, the enemy hung, for he received just judgment for his deeds. Those others who were wicked also received a similar fate, judgment and death, and were no more. Those who were victorious lived, empowered and recalled the greatest thing God could have bestowed upon any one of them: life. The cycle of life was held in the hands of a woman, Esther, the life-bearer, standing as a long-term reminder in the feast of Purim. Just as the resurrection was for all who would be saved, Purim was for all, as well, as all were called to hear the word of the festival, women along with the men, because Purim specifically involved women. In the specifics of Purim: the timing, the feasting, and the reminder that it was for all, we hear the promise of the resurrection to come, that God would bring us all from death to life, and that it would come through a redemptive sacrifice.

## **Esther 10:1-4**

***King Xerxes imposed tribute throughout the empire, to its distant shores. And all his acts of power and might, together with a full account of the greatness of Mordecai to which the king had raised him, are they not written in the book of the annals of the kings of Media and Persia? Mordecai the Jew was second in rank to King Xerxes, preeminent among the Jews, and held in high esteem by his many fellow Jews, because he worked for the good of his people and spoke up for the welfare of all the Jews.***

(Related Bible references: Psalm 18:35, Ezra 4:15, Isaiah 26:12, 2

Corinthians 3:1-6)

The book of Esther began without its namesake. The book of Esther also ends without its namesake. Throughout, we can recognize and feel her presence. Esther is the center of the book, the heart of it; the love of it. It is much like the way the Scriptures themselves center Christ. There are other people and other characters in the Scriptures, but the center of them all is Christ, Himself. Even though Esther is not mentioned in the end, what happens at the end of the book could not have ever been accomplished without the work of Esther. Her legacy, her work lived on, even while still living and active in the successes of King Xerxes, who was obedient in responding to what needed to be done. It lived on in Mordecai, who although a man able to stand on his own, rose to authority because of Esther's intervention and positioning within the Kingdom.

Sometimes we think that to leave our mark or influence others we must have our name splashed everywhere and be the constant center of attention. This is the opposite of the profundity that marks spiritual types, those opportunities by which we embrace our spot to point to something greater and more profound than we are by ourselves. By allowing ourselves to become types, we are participating in the plan of salvation in an entirely different and new way: we are walking in and living it, experiencing it up close and personal, in a way that we cannot if we simply stand back and observe. Belief is wonderful, but belief should be more than just doctrine in our minds and words on paper. By becoming types, we are participants, recognizing times and seasons, and rising to stand for our Lord as we assume that position of letting God show as the priority through us.

*Are we starting to commend ourselves again? Or we do not, like some [false teachers], need written credentials or letters of recommendation to you or from you, [do we]?*

*[No] you yourselves are our letter of recommendation (our credentials), written in your hearts, to be known (perceived, recognized) and read by everybody.*

*You show and make obvious that you are a letter from Christ delivered by us, not written with ink but with [the] Spirit of [the] living God, not on tablets of stone but on tablets of human hearts.*

*Such is the reliance and confidence that we have through Christ toward and with reference to God.*

*Not that we are fit (qualified and sufficient in ability) of ourselves to form personal judgments or to claim or count anything as coming from us, but our power and ability and sufficiency are from God.*

*[It is He] Who has qualified us [making us to be fit and worthy and sufficient] as ministers and dispensers of a new covenant [of salvation through Christ], not [ministers] of the letter (of legally written code) but of the Spirit; for the code [of the Law] kills, but the [Holy] Spirit makes alive.*
(2 Corinthians 3:1-6, AMPC)

The power of operating as a living letter, or a living type, being read (observed) of all people proves the work of the Spirit as alive, whereas the work of the Law kills. The difference is the purpose. The purpose of the Spirit is to give life; after all, the Spirit is, indeed, the life-giver. The purpose of the written law was to alert to death, to make us aware of the very need for the Savior in the first place, and to aware us that no matter our best efforts, we were never going to find life without divine intervention. The point of a type is to reveal that divine intervention, God's divine intention to the world, reminding others of God's true love and care for humanity. Now, as believers, we are called to stand as types ourselves, pointing to the realities that we know exist, but are not always visible, showing little bits and pieces of God's love to the entire world. As types, we become that encounter: something that points to something else, something greater, and lets them know that He is still there, and He still cares. It is being willing to take on that spiritual nature to reveal God to people who may not even realize they are missing Him in some way.

Ruth revealed God to her mother-in-law who, rightfully speaking, should have been the one to reveal God to Ruth, at least according to the hardness and indifference of the law. Ruth revealed God because Naomi was in a place stricken by grief, where she couldn't see or experience God for herself. It was easier to believe that God had nothing more for her then to see through to the next day and trust that something was coming, even if it wasn't visible. Naomi saw her life, her culture, and assumed God was done with her, too. As Ruth lived a faith she didn't understand, she showed Naomi a divine promise, that God was real and faithful in the face of loss, and, then she and her mother-in-law became a type of the church.

Ruth also revealed God to Boaz through a sacrificial sense of love and commitment shown to Naomi. Boaz might have known faith and religion in a literal sense, but watching the commitment that Ruth made to Naomi revealed God to him in a way that he'd never experienced prior. He knew business, he knew how to interact in righteousness, and we can see from the Scriptures that he knew how to treat his workers well, but he hadn't seen anyone make such a profound and lasting commitment to someone else with no legal or moral obligation to do so. By standing as she did, Ruth revealed God to Boaz, too.

Vashti revealed God to Xerxes to the point it infuriated him. Vashti opened a door through self-respect and self-esteem, standing against a bossy, demeaning, and drunk man who didn't know how to honor anyone but himself. By standing up to Xerxes, Vashti revealed himself to him, that he was making an idol of himself, and he did not know how to properly be a ruler or a husband to anyone. Vashti let Xerxes know that he had to challenge and change, and as he dealt with four years of heavy and frustrating battle, he came to deal with the realities of himself. Maybe it didn't come like he expected, but it prepared him to live and deal with Esther in a different manner than he had done so with Vashti.

Esther revealed God to Xerxes as well, but in a different way. Xerxes might have been mighty in battle, but he wasn't aware of what was going on among his own administration. He wasn't seeing Haman for who he was, and he was right under his nose. Blinded by Haman's familial status, prestige, and wealth, he simply assumed that Haman was doing right by him. Esther revealed important priorities to Xerxes as a leader and her heart to him as a Jewish woman, one who couldn't bear to see her entire nation annihilated.

Esther also revealed God to the Jewish people, as well as to Mordecai, all of whom were able to see God's plan work through her. Esther stepped up and did a job that wasn't easy to do, that had the potential to put her in the death seat, so to speak. By doing what Esther did, she let the Jews of Persia know that God was still with them, even though they were not currently living where their ancestors did. God was still God, He transcends all time and space, and He was still their God, no matter where they may be. She also gave everyone who helped her the confidence and assurance of knowing there is no job too big or too small in the Kingdom of God, and that we should never put down someone's contribution as being too small. Not everyone could be Esther, not everyone could be Mordecai, but everyone who prayed, fasted, sent messages back and forth, encouraged, and stood behind and assisted the woman of God were all just as important in the eyes of God as she was.

Both the books of Ruth and Esther shows us so powerfully how one person can make a difference in the lives of many, just by accepting divine assignment. By becoming a type, by showing forth the impact that God has had on one's life (even if we don't always understand it fully for ourselves), we can see that God can reveal - and do - amazing things through our own obedience. As we team up with others - with the "queer kids" that no one else wants to connect with – the outcasts, the transgender individuals, the queer platonic partnerships, the asexuals, the gays, the widows, the lonely, the lost, and the hurting – God does powerful things as we work together. We talk about wanting to change the world, but the reality of types and shadows is that we don't just walk in and change the world. No, we start by changing ourselves, allowing God to display His wonder and might through us. We live differently, touching all we meet, choosing to do what seems different, unconventional, or impossible, regardless of gender, following in the footsteps of our heroines of faith. We follow a divinely led instinct, a witness of the Spirit, and follow it unto the end of touching heaven and changing the earth around us. May these women – and the types they provide – encourage all of us to step up and step out, to seek out our spirituality in our actions and everyday lives and open the door through our behavior to show others that little bit of God that maybe they (and any situation at large) are missing.

# REFERENCES

**Epigraph**
[1]Compiled by Ann Marie Imbornoni. "Quotations by Women." https://www.infoplease.com/quotations-women. Accessed August 21, 2018.

**Introduction**
- "Book Of Ruth." https://en.wikipedia.org/wiki/Book_of_Ruth. Accessed July 9, 2018.
- "Book of Esther." https://en.wikipedia.org/wiki/Book_of_Esther. Accessed July 9, 2018.
- "Five Megillot." https://en.wikipedia.org/wiki/Five_Megillot. Accessed July 9, 2018.
- "Ketuvim." https://en.wikipedia.org/wiki/Ketuvim. Accessed July 9, 2018.
- "Mordecai." https://en.wikipedia.org/wiki/Mordecai. Accessed July 9, 2018.
- "Samuel." https://en.wikipedia.org/wiki/Samuel. Accessed July 9, 2018.

**Chapter 1**
[1]*Strong's Exhaustive Concordance of the Bible*, #7458
[2]Ibid., #4124
[3]Ibid., #0458
[4]Ibid., #5281
[5]Ibid., #4248
[6]Ibid., #3630
[7]Ibid., #7327
[8]Ibid., #6204
[9]Ibid., #0517
[10]Ibid., #1004
[11]Ibid., #2617
[12]Ibid., #1035
[13]Ibid., #4755
[14]Ibid., #7489
[15]Ibid., #8184
[16]Ibid., #7105
[17]Burton, Judd H. "Chemosh: the Ancient God of the Moabites."

https://www.thoughtco.com/chemosh-lord-of-the-moabites-117630. Accessed July 17, 2018.

## Chapter 2
[1] *Strong's Exhaustive Concordance of the Bible*, #4129
[2] Ibid., #4940
[3] Ibid., #0458
[4] Ibid., #1162
[5] Ibid., #3950
[6] Ibid., #1323
[7] Ibid., #2580
[8] Ibid., #5237
[9] Ibid., #2620
[10] Ibid., #5162
[11] Ibid., #1288
[12] Ibid., #1288

## Chapter 3
[1] *Strong's Exhaustive Concordance of the Bible*, #4494
[2] Ibid., #2219
[3] Ibid., #1637
[4] Ibid., #7364
[5] Ibid., #5480
[6] Ibid., #0519
[7] Ibid., #6566
[8] Ibid., #3671
[9] Ibid., #2428
[10] Ibid., #0802
[11] Ibid., #4304
[12] Ibid., #7387
[13] "Ruth." http://www.biblecustoms.org/bishop-kc-pillai/old-and-new-testament-orientalisms/ruth. Accessed July 27, 2018.

## Chapter 4
[1] *Strong's Exhaustive Concordance of the Bible*, #2205
[2] Ibid., #5275
[3] Ibid., #5707
[4] Ibid., #0672
[5] Ibid., #6557
[6] Ibid., #8559
[7] Ibid., #3063
[8] Ibid., #5744
[9] Ibid., #3445
[10] Ibid., #1732
[11] "Where does the custom of "tossing of the sandal" in Ruth come from Why/how does it come to symbolize a successful business transaction?" https://judaism.stackexchange.com/questions/76428/where-does-the-custom-of-the-tossing-of-the-sandal-in-ruth-come-from-why-how. Accessed July 28, 2018.
[12] "Perez (Son of Judah)." https://en.wikipedia.org/wiki/Perez_(son_of_Judah).

Accessed July 28, 2018.

## Chapter 5
[1] *Strong's Exhaustive Concordance of the Bible*, #0325
[2] Ibid., #7800
[3] Ibid., #6539
[4] Ibid., #4074
[5] Ibid., #4960
[6] Ibid., #2060
[7] Ibid., #4436
[8] Ibid., #5631
[9] Ibid., #2450
[10] Ibid., #0802
[11] Ibid., #959
[12] Ibid., #3366
[13] Ibid., #1167
[14] Ibid., #8323
[15] "Religion of the Persian Empire, The." https://estherslegacy.com/tag/religion-of-xerxes/. Accessed July 30, 2018.
[16] "Achaemenid Empire." https://en.wikipedia.org/wiki/Achaemenid_Empire. Accessed July 30, 2018.

## Chapter 6
[1] *Strong's Exhaustive Concordance of the Bible*, #0310
[2] Ibid., #1004
[3] Ibid., #0802
[4] Ibid., #1896
[5] Ibid., #8562
[6] Ibid., #3190
[7] Ibid., #4782
[8] Ibid., #1540
[9] Ibid., #5019
[10] Ibid., #3204
[11] Ibid., #1919
[12] Ibid., #0635
[13] Ibid., #8190
[14] Ibid., #6370
[15] Ibid., #7121
[16] Ibid., #3947
[17] Ibid., #1323
[18] Ibid., #0157
[19] Ibid., #0904
[20] Ibid., #8657
[21] Ibid., #6086
[22] Ibid., #5162
[23] Ibid., #1697
[24] Marino, Lee Ann B. *Ministering to LGBTs – And Those Who Love Them.* "Chapter 9: The Biblical Eunuch." Raleigh, North Carolina: Apostolic University Press, 2016.
[25] Ibid.

## Chapter 7
[1] *Strong's Exhaustive Concordance of the Bible*, #2001
[2] Ibid., #4099
[3] Ibid., #0091
[4] Ibid., #3766
[5] Ibid., #6332
[6] Ibid., #2885
[7] Ibid., #0323
[8] Ibid., #0006
[9] Ibid., #8242
[10] Ibid., #0665
[11] Ibid., #4428
[12] Ibid., #8179
[13] Ibid., #6685
[14] Ibid., #1065
[15] Ibid., #4553
[16] Ibid., #2047
[17] Ibid., #2020
[18] Ibid., #6256
[19] Ibid., #0006
[20] Ibid., #7218
[21] Ibid., #8275
[22] Ibid., #2238
[23] Ibid., #0157
[24] Ibid., #7737
[25] Ibid., #0157
[26] Ibid., #0057

## Chapter 8
[1] *Strong's Exhaustive Concordance of the Bible*, #7596
[2] Ibid., #6862
[3] Ibid., #0341
[4] Ibid., #3533
[5] Ibid., #2726
[6] Ibid., #8056
[7] Ibid., #6577
[8] Ibid., #1813
[9] Ibid., #0630
[10] Ibid., #6334
[11] Ibid., #0118
[12] Ibid., #0743
[13] Ibid., #6534
[14] Ibid., #0747
[15] Ibid., #0742
[16] Ibid., #2055
[17] Ibid., #6332
[18] Ibid., 8533
[19] Ibid., #7965
[20] Ibid., #0571
[21] "Purim How-To Guide."

https://www.chabad.org/holidays/purim/article_cdo/aid/1362/jewish/Purim-How-To-Guide.htm. Accessed August 14, 2018.

# ABOUT THE AUTHOR
Dr. Lee Ann B. Marino, Ph.D., D.Min., D.D.

**DR. LEE ANN B. MARINO, PH.D., D.MIN., D.D.** (she/her) is "everyone's favorite theologian" leading Gen X, Millennials, and Gen Z with expertise in leadership training, queer and feminist theology, general religion, and apostolic theology. She has served in ministry since 1998 and was ordained as a pastor in 2002 and an apostle in 2010. She founded what is now Sanctuary Apostolic Fellowship Empowerment (SAFE) Ministries in 2004. Under her ministry heading Dr. Marino is founder and Overseer of Sanctuary International Fellowship Tabernacle (SIFT) (the original home of National Coming Out Sunday) and The Sanctuary Network, and Chancellor of Apostolic Covenant Theological Seminary (ACTS).

Affectionately nicknamed "the Spitfire," Dr. Marino has spent over two decades as an "apostle, preacher, and teacher" (2 Timothy 1:11), exercising her personal mandate to become "all things to all people" (1 Corinthians 9:22). Her embrace of spiritual issues (both technical and intimate) has found its home among both seekers and believers, those who desire spiritual answers to today's issues.

Dr. Marino has preached throughout the United States, Puerto Rico, and Europe in hundreds of religious services and experiences throughout the years. A history maker in her own right, she has spent over two decades in advocacy, education, and work for and within minority spiritual communities (including African American, Hispanic, and LGBTQ+). She has also served as the first woman on all-male synods, councils, and panels, as well as the first preacher or speaker welcomed of a different race, sexual orientation, or identity among diverse communities. Today, Dr. Marino's work extends to over 150 countries as she hosts the popular *Kingdom Now* podcast, which is in the top 20 percentile of all podcasts worldwide. She is also the author of over 35 books and the popular Patheos column, *Leadership on Fire*. To date, she has had five bestselling titles within their subject matter: *Understanding Demonology, Spiritual Warfare, Healing, and Deliverance: A Manual for the Christian Minister*; *Ministry School Boot Camp: Training for Helps Ministries, Appointments, and Beyond*; *Discovering Intimacy: A Journey Through the Song of Solomon*; *Fruit of the Vine: Study and Commentary on the Fruit of the Spirit*; and *Ministering to LGBTQ+ (and Those Who Love Them): A Primer for Queer Theology* (and its accompanying workbook).

As a public icon and social media influencer, Dr. Marino advocates healthy body image (curvy/full-figured), representation as a demisexual/aromantic, and albinism awareness as a model. Known to those she works with, she is a spiritual mom, teacher, leader, professor, confidant, and friend. She continues to transform, receiving new teaching, revelation, and insight in this thing we call "ministry." Through years of spiritual growth and maturity, Dr. Marino stands as herself, here to present what God has given to her for any who have an ear to hear.

For more information, visit her website at kingdompowernow.org.

www.ingramcontent.com/pod-product-compliance
Lightning Source LLC
LaVergne TN
LVHW051116080426
835510LV00018B/2069